# SAIL IT FLAT

# SAIL IT FLAT
## The Sunfish Racing Primer

by Larry Lewis
with Chuck Millican

Illustrations by Mark Smith

Chicago
Quadrangle Books
One-Design & Offshore Yachtsman

Library of Congress Catalog Card Number: 78-182206
International Standard Book Number: 0-8129-0238-6

**To Brownie**

# CONTENTS

# SAIL IT FLAT

# INTRODUCTION

Seventy five thousand Sunfish sailors can't be wrong. The AMF—Alcort Company, seller of the largest number of one-design boats in the history of the sailboat business, has developed the biggest group of nautical enthusiasts in the yachting field. This manual is for them — the novice and the salty. Hopefully we will draw the interest of other small boat sailors too.

The book is rather loosely structured although the recurrent theme is how some of us prepare for the most purely one-design regattas of them all: The Sunfish World Championships.

The point we will try to make is that with adequate preparation and plenty of practice new sailors can become competent in this highly entertaining sport.

The steps we take to get ready for a World's Championship are carefully documented here. It is often said that regattas are

Chuck Millican

won on the beach. While gadgetry is more elaborate on some other dinghies, the amount of tuning we give a Sunfish will simply astound many experienced sailors who think of the boat as a very simple plastic toy.

After some chapters on preparing ourselves and our boats, we will relate our experiences on how to make the boat go fast on certain points of sailing. Needless to say, we draw on the ideas of a number of our friends and regular competitors. While basic principles are roughly the same in all dinghies, each is different from the other in tuning and handling. We have some observations in these pages which we don't believe have been incorporated in any other "how to" sailing book.

We also offer some comments on team racing techniques. Chuck and I were privileged to sail for the 1971 Sunfish National and World team race champions and we think that out of these experiences we have some fresh ideas to offer. Team racing is more fun than any other outdoor sport and through these pages we hope to translate our enthusiasm for this exciting and exacting game.

As we write these words, the temperature is 16 above and the wind from the Northwest at 15 gusting to 29. We are not, however, hibernating for the winter. We sail tomorrow. Frost-biting has become a very popular activity, in the Northeast at least. If you dress adequately, it sure beats staying at home on a weekend doing the chores you hadn't gotten around to while you were sailing in the summer and fall. We will try to make some suggestions for frostbiting which will enhance your enjoyment of the sport; what you are going to do about the chores remains your own problems.

Finally we devote some time to the methods of repairing your boat. I don't profess to be an expert but Chuck has rebuilt so many boats that he has developed plenty of know-how. He also worked for Alcort and has had an opportunity to learn first hand how the manufacturer repairs boats. The satisfaction that arises from sailing a boat in good order which you have personally repaired gives much pleasure in itself. If you follow the advice given here, the Sunfish will last a good long time, confirming the theory that it is yachting's best investment.

The Sunfish is, after all, the vehicle which so many of us have used to perpetuate our enjoyment of sailing. Never has a sailboat created so much fun for so many people.

**Larry Lewis**

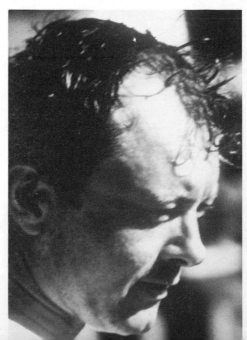

Garry Hoyt, 1970 Sunfish World's Champion

# TRAINING

I have just come in from running over my 1.1 mile cross country course with my glasses steamed over and sweat pants speckled with sleet. I have been training for two months and I still stagger on the last hill. Yet this running and the forms of physical training the others will undergo is what will make us competitive.

We run because we think we achieve stamina from the activity. Normal championship courses are, as in the Olympics, triangle, windward, leeward, windward. In heavy breezes stamina is a most important factor. The great Long Island Sound light air sailors, who can't hike out flat with many pounds of wet clothes on their backs, don't have the consistent speed necessary in fresh winds.

I also run, I think, because of the smug feeling it gives me; one feels so superior when he is capable of running a mile in six minutes.

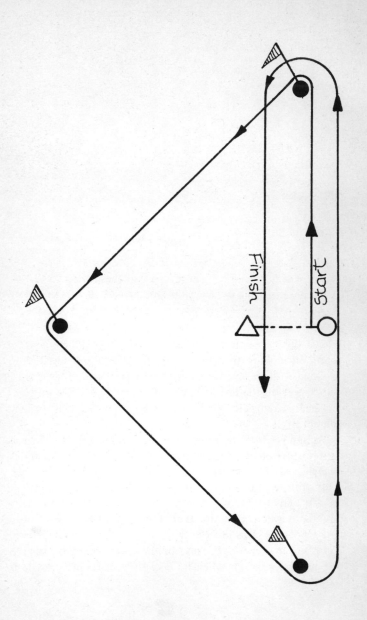

Jeorg Bruder

We hear of various training techniques others use. Valentin Mankin, of Russia, 1968 Olympic Gold Medalist in Finns, is supposed to do 25 right arm push ups and then duplicate the feat with his left arm. This usually achieves the desired effect of sending the less dedicated back to the bar from whence they came the night before.

Jeorg Bruder's feats of strength are legendary. We understand he does 100 situps with a 90 pound weight on his back as a nightly exercise. This chore is not mandatory to win a Long Island Sound club race, but we assure you that if he hadn't developed his fantastic strength, we wouldn't be including the following anecdote:

Jeorg had never won a Finn Gold Cup, but he had been runner up twice. As he approached the final leeward mark of the last race of the 1969 Gold Cup in Bermuda he had only to hold his position on the beat to maintain a third second place finish. His mainsheet block broke, which would have finished most of us, as this particular race was being sailed at the tail end of Hurricane Inga. Jeorg simply horsed the boat all the way upwind without the mechanical advantage of the series of blocks and held on against some of the world's really super athletes.

We understand that after one year of Olympic training, Garry Hoyt's whole physique changed dramatically. We think Garry won the 1970 World's because of absolute physical superiority. There was no one except Jeorg Bruder who could create any competition for him on the rigorous 25-knot three race second day; and we are not deprecating the other efforts Garry goes to.

Why strength and stamina? When racing in a good breeze, you must be able to tack countless times with speed and precision. You've got to have the strength left to harden up smoothly at turning marks. You must be able to sheet in hard in a breeze. Controlling a broaching or wildly planing Sunfish off wind is physically very demanding; just look at the picture on page 14. Most important you must be mentally alert enough to concentrate on tactics rather than how tired you are.

There are many training devices used to get the champions in shape. Look at the hiking bench on the next page. This is a device popularized by Paul Elvstrom. It simulates on dry land the tortures you go through on the water when you are hiked out. Sitting on the hiking bench doing situps with weights on your back is just the trick to tone up those thigh and stomach muscles.

Plans for the hiking machine are included on page 85. The total cost of the one we made did not exceed three dollars. My leg strap is adjustable. It came off the rear seat of the family automobile. It makes a very nice place to hook the feet for all sizes and ages of hikers. Alcort should consider installing an adjustable hiking strap in the center of the cockpit of the Sunfish; at present shorter sailors are at a handicap. The fittings could be molded right into the cockpit.

A regular exercise regimen such as the Royal Canadian Air Force exercises makes a real contribution to stamina and quickness. AMF—Voit has at least three tools to help you improve the physical skills used in sailing. The Jiffy-Gym is a wide thick rubber band you stretch apart. It helps build up shoulder and chest muscles. The Exergrip helps improve your

**The Jiffy Gym — Good for all sexes**

grip, as does the hand exerciser which also strengthens the fingers and forearms.

In the final analysis, the dedication involved in sailing the boat flat in a big breeze is what training is all about. In the first minutes off the starting line, you are frequently going boat for boat with others. The sailor who can keep the boat level, concentrating on his sail and the tactical situations without coming up for a breather, will break clear.

But in a Sunfish, training becomes important for other reasons too. The Sunfish is a "weight boat". It is under-canvased, or under-Dacroned if you wish. Weight plays a tremendous part in the game. Not as an excuse mind you, but when the wind drops down and marginal planing conditions exist you would do better to put your daughter in the boat. Upwind in 20 knots the agile 200 pounder is back in the ball game. Under 15 knots and watch Herve Roche, the 135 pound South American champion, ride those waves. He will pass you to weather, to leeward or right over you.

Notice that in the picture, right, Herve has very little of his boat in the water as he is immediately accelerating into a plane upon rounding the weather mark. The reduced wetted surface he achieves because of his comparatively light weight gives him a tremendous advantage on reaching legs in particular.

Weight is a disadvantage because it keeps you from planing in marginal conditions. The biggest chunks of yardage gained or lost in racing come in off wind sailing. The boat that is planing can gain fantastic amounts on the boat that wallows. Also, acceleration after a tack or after being struck by a large wave is directly proportional to weight.

Ding Schoonmaker, multi class champion, has commented that to be competitive a Finn must be tacked in three seconds flat out to flat out. The Sunfish is no different. When you consider the narrow overlap situations that frequently determine the ultimate outcome of small boat racing, you realize the importance of seconds. The person who can gain a second a tack has that much advantage on the fleet. In the normal

range of sailing conditions a weight area of 165 pounds seems ideal.

If you simply cannot take the time from whatever you are doing to don sweat clothes and work out, we have a very good exercise for you. Each morning when you are standing in the subway reading your "Times", lean casually against a door with your feet apart about 12 inches and about 18 inches out from the door. Keep your back straight. Now begin a slow descent, bending your knees and keeping your back flat against the door. When your thighs are at right angles to your calves, hold the position for a couple of subway stops. This will strengthen your hiking muscles in just the manner needed. Chances are you won't look any more peculiar than the rest of the subway riders either.

# HEAVY WEATHER CLOTHES

When the wind pipes up to a fresh breeze what should all of us Diet Pepsi drinkers do after getting in shape for the marginal planing conditions? The answer is simple — wear wet cotton clothes.

The 1970 World's was a convocation of teddy bears. You have never seen such a conglomerate of spindly legs over-burdened with stuffed torsos. But with reason. You can always put weight on but you cannot take it off. There are a number of versions, but here is what I do to gain weight.

I wear a standard cotton T shirt. Then I put on a snug fitting Flotherchoc. Naturally, there are several other good life jackets, such as the Elvstrom and the GenTex, but I am ac-customed to the Flotherchoc. This is a flexible life saving vest composed of 250 or so plastic airfilled bubbles in a nylon fabric shell. It is an easy, comfortable garment to wear and I judge it to have saved my life on at least one occasion. It is

warm in the winter and cool in the summer. The Flotherchoc is mandatory with us regardless of whether a race committee specifies one to be worn or carried aboard. We would never sail without it.

Naturally this should be covered up as explained on page 26. I next put on a cotton sweat shirt with the sleeves cut off at the shoulders. Sweat shirts should be sleeveless because when the inevitable capsize occurs, you can raise your arms out of the water unencumbered with excess weight and swim for your boat.

Next I wear a garment composed of four or five no-sleeve sweat shirts. Simply chop off the sleeves at the shoulders and the remaining shirts are put one inside the other. Cut them all straight down the front and insert three brass grommets on either side. With nylon line to secure the fronts, you have a sweat shirt jacket, relatively easy to dry, but quick to absorb water and add an additional 10 pounds or so. The garment may not be too handsome, but it is practical. (Our Sears bills for repairing the washing machine due to the nylon cords fouling the works have amounted to the original cost of 23 new sweat shirts. Don't wash them, hang them up to dry.)

Some people go to the extra trouble of neatly stitching their jacket; it is neater but the jacket does not dry as quickly. Add one more tight short sleeve shirt over the whole mess to contain any drooping cloth or lines which might serve as a drag when you are hiked full out. Now you have seven wet shirts and at least 15 pounds. Another legal method of gaining weight is to wear cotton sweat pants. Teddy Moore will wear as many as seven pairs of sweat pants. Harvey Howell, who races in Puerto Rico, cuts off his sweat pants and makes shorts of them. This makes sense as it gives freedom to his legs and keeps the weight where you really want it. Carl Knight puts pieces of carpet in the seat of his pants which not only helps him gain weight but is more comfortable. Heavy turkish towels around the shoulders are an excellent absorber of water.

Mike Shaw reckons that he adds as much as 60 pounds of wet clothes. You better not have back trouble and be engaged in this activity as this puts a real strain on the lower back.

Notice in the picture, right, that one of the competitors is wearing his life jacket on the outside. I don't know how many people have experienced the sensation of having the boom come whipping over on a tack, only to have it catch in their life vest, causing a capsize. To eliminate this problem, you wear a shirt over the jacket regardless of the breeze.

Notice that all three sailors in the foreground are wearing gloves. For someone unused to sailing in the Caribbean, gloves are recommended. The sun can burn your lily white hands so badly that it is pure torture to sheet in. Finally notice that Ken Klein, who is wearing his complement of wet sweat shirts plus beard, is holding the boat most level.

Henry Sprague and Peter Barrett staged a protest to determine the legality of wearing extra ballast in wet sweat shirt

form. NAYRU Appeal decision number 109 upheld the wearer of the wet cotton cloth.

But remember, wear as little as you can possibly get away with and still hold the boat flat; the Sunfish is after all a "weight" boat.

One thing you should not skimp on is footwear. Sperry Topsider moccasins do an excellent job of helping you retain your footing. They are "de rigueur" in the evening at formal yachting parties in the islands.

In many climates hats are important. A standard white crew hat is good. Bill Gleason, former O.K. Dinghy champion of Thailand, and current Sunfish class leader from Puerto Rico, has the answer: To keep hats on in a breeze, wrinkle up your forehead and screw on the cap; sometimes it's the only way.

# TRAVEL PLANNING

Those long winter nights are made warmer through the anticipation of a Caribbean regatta. The fun you can have in preparing your travel kit, training, even dieting, frequently is as enjoyable as the actual series. Here are some of the things we might do to prepare for any regatta, but particularly one in the islands.

Many regattas do not offer brand new boats. Some do not offer competitive equipment at all. These boats, however, are either loaned outright or rented at very nominal fees. Materials to repair borrowed boats are now more readily available. The dealer in Puerto Rico recently had a superb stock of parts, but the prices in the islands are high.

Make sure you bring a bailing plug, gasket and marble. I always do after an experience I had several years ago. During the opening race of the 1966 Caribbean Championships, we sailed in rather unprotected water and the sea was really working up. My bailer was corroded and did not work; the cockpit became full of water. My boat just would not tack in those big seas as water continued to slosh over the lip of the cockpit. I finally had to jibe to get onto the other tack. The Sunfish bailer is quite satisfactory only when you can unscrew it. In big seas I take the plug completely out both upwind and down.

Bring plenty of horizontal hinge pins. I hope I will not be accused of Agnewism or Hooverism if I say that you should remove every detachable part of your boat at night. Rudder pins seem to go fast. Another item that disappears quickly when there is a big sea is a Clorox bottle bailer. You should bring your own.

Bring your own sheet. New Sunfish come equipped with Dacron sheets, but many of the older boats still have the original standard cotton sheet. Cotton work gloves with plastic dots can save a significant amount of trouble with your hands. The main thing about gloves is that they should protect your hands but not restrict your dexterity or grip.

Boards, rudders and sails are not regularly supplied by the gracious lenders of the boats. Bring your own cleats — swivel variety, cam, clam or ratchet. I think it proper to leave them on the boat after the series.

Most clubs have electrical outlets, but for Sunfish purposes, a hand drill works fine and should be a part of the kit. Do not forget bits. Remember bolts and cap nuts for the rudder and tiller fittings. Also, bring plenty of tape, a screw driver, wrenches, pliers, a knife, Orlon or Nylon yarn for tell tales, outhaul line, a spun polyester halyard, a sponge and even some detergent. Caribbean beaches have oil on them too, sad to say.

We have prepared a Regatta Checklist which you will find on page 111. Reference to this will save you the embarrassment of showing up at a regatta someday without some minor piece of equipment such as the mast, a sail, etc. Don't laugh, it happens to everybody.

Don't carry knives on board the plane; check them through. You don't want to be mistaken for a hijacker. With the costumes most sailors wear, it's a wonder the airlines will carry us at all.

If you are flying get to the airport early. Even if you have a confirmed seat, Caribbean flights in the winter will go with standbys if you don't show up an hour in advance. Pan Am will now confirm and mail tickets to your home as long as you pay your phone bills on time. That's right, just call from home and they will mail and charge them to you. Other airlines probably will too.

Check the shot requirements. Most of the places where we sail Sunfish don't require shots. Venezuela does demand a smallpox vaccination. Get it early, sometimes they "take". Get a tourist card at the carrier's office in advance; it's easier than having them do it for you 10 minutes before flight time.

Most countries on the Sunfish circuit do not require passports. Venezuela does not either but definite proof of citizenship is required. A passport is simple and the best.

When you arrive at your destination, reconfirm your return reservation at the airport. Write on your ticket envelope the name of the agent who reconfirmed you. Sunday night in February in the San Juan airport is like the same night in August on the Long Island Expressway. The competitive and nefarious ways in all of us come out when Eastern, American and Pan Am are one plane short back to New York.

In all the islands accommodations in the homes of the local sailors can usually be provided. Sailors are a warm bunch and if you need a bed, they will always find one for you. Room at the mark the next day? That's another story. Some of the best friendships we have made have been as a result of the regattas we have sailed in Bermuda, Puerto Rico, St. Thomas and Venezuela. After all, the ultimate reason for racing Sunfish is fun. I am sure a lot of other classes have fine people, but it is hard to imagine a better crowd than those who campaign the Sunfish.

# DAGGERBOARDS

It is highly probable that AMF—Alcort will undertake the high initial expense of creating molds from which to manufacture plastic rudders and daggerboards. While perhaps not as cosmetically appealing as the mahogany currently used, the synthetic material would be far more durable than wood. Still even if AMF—Alcort does take this step there will be 200,000 boards and rudders left around and it is for their owners that we write these next two chapters.

Your physical training is now behind you. When you open the box containing your new boat, slice off the tape holding the wooden components and feel them. Immediately you will know what one of your first tasks is going to be.

At the '70 World's we listened to runner-up Mike Shaw, Jack Evans and Dick Griffin debate the hydrodynamic aspects of the Sunfish board. The theory is that a blunted, rounded forward edge bulging out and then tapering gradually back to a sharpish after edge would produce the most even flow of water off the surface of the board.

The class rules prescribe that the boards may neither be planed or shaped, but the lively discussion we heard led us to believe that an awful lot of legal sanding is going on.

Regardless of whether the edges should be razor sharp, blunt or rounded, unquestionably the board must be smooth. That is legal. Normal Alcort varnishing is too "mass produced" for our taste. Most of us will sand down the board and rudder, then refinish. Dick Griffin uses Helmsman Graphspeed, a polyurethane coating mixed with graphite. This surface is extremely smooth and may be the best available finish.

Bryce Suydam, the Great South Bay king, paints his board white with an epoxy paint. Bryce knows the value of detecting weed promptly after growing up on that water-covered weed patch. Against a white background it is easier to spot any foreign matter trailing from your rudder or board. Actually you really cannot see your board from a normal sailing position and the white background is only important on the rudder. However it is more aesthetically pleasing to have both wooden parts painted the same color.

I paint my board with a clear polyurethane which fills dents and then wet sand, wet sand, wet sand. When I have too deep scratches and dents I fill them with Marine Tex and resand; it does a beautiful job. And is a smooth board important? Garry Hoyt thinks so: I can remember the lunch break before the final race for the 1970 Caribbean Championship. The bulk of us were around the ice bucket gulping Cokes and other beverages. Garry was around the corner wet sanding his board; Garry won.

Alcort should provide a template for board and rudder. We are told that the board and rudder comprise about 15% of the wetted surface of the boat. This is a tremendous amount of area not to care for properly; it is also a great portion which if shaped can create dramatic improvement in speed, particularly in acceleration after tacking. While ethics are a part of the issue, what are you going to do if you crash into rocks and must sand or plane the jagged edges of a board? A template would salve everybody's conscience.

After brushing the mahogany dust out of our hair, we might as well do some more things to the board while still in the shop. Screw a small brass eye into the forward part of the cap on the daggerboard. A shock cord attached to this eye from the halyard block will hold the board in any elevated position you desire. Some people have extended a shock cord to the interlocking eyebolts on the spars — this holds the sail out on downwind legs in light air. We are sure, however, that the intent of the rule permitting shock cords is for the sole purpose of restraining the daggerboard — not for uses such as a J.C. strap.

Some people mark the board so that they know when the tip is just showing below the trunk. We think this has merit but we find that we vary the amount of immersion of the board according to the wind, sea and current conditions. The board should be up as far as it will go while still providing steerage and balance.

The subject of chattering boards is a dilemma in itself. Possibly the warp of the board determines the chatter. For sure, vibration is undesirable. We guarantee that when your speed picks up and your board begins to chatter, you are not reaching your maximum potential. To avoid a warped board keep it out of the sun when not in use.

Bob Bowles paints his board with fiberglass resin around that part contained in the trunk when the board is full down. That may be the answer. Most of us experiment with boards until we find one that doesn't chatter.

It is possible that the answer may be to load up the trunk with epoxy in a form fitting mold around the daggerboard. Skip Cook tried this with some success. Make sure you carefully wrap the board in wax paper, however, or you will never get it out. This might achieve a really stable effect. When one of our boats gets really old we may try this technique.

We know there must be people who make their boards into jibing boards. Essentially this is a board which is cocked to weather by putting a wedge at the windward trailing edge. Just a couple of degrees of angle would make a difference.

We have never seen this technique in action to our knowledge. We know it is definitely illegal. The rule which permits centerboard holding devices was designed for restraining the board, not to create a jibing board for upwind sailing.

Basically you use just as little board as possible. We even suggest that you don't need full board upwind in drifter conditions. In fluky stuff when a puff comes you should pull up the board to get motion underway. Experiment with raising the board in very heavy winds. The reduced lateral resistance created by a board a few inches up may enable you to foot faster and cancel out the pointing ability generated by a board full down.

Finally, keep the board smooth and the edges clean and free from splinters.

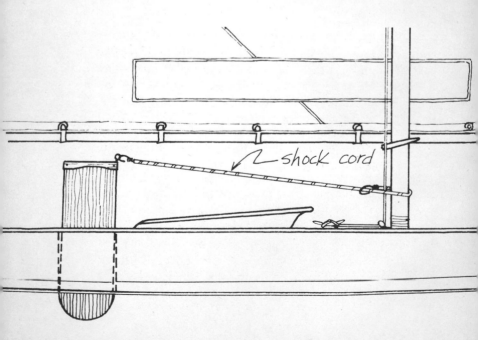

# RUDDER AND TILLER

Less attention is given to the rudder than the board in most sailing books; however, one of the most significant factors in slowing the boat is poor rudder control. Most of us tend to tense up under the duress of competition and either move the tiller too much or clutch it at any angle in a death grip, intent on what's up ahead. The Sunfish rudder, smallish though it may be, still will stall when it goes beyond six or seven degrees. There are, however, some good ways to improve the contribution of the rudder.

Bob Johnstone, one of the original Sunfish leaders, suggested some additions to the latch plate which will be discussed later. We have borrowed from Bob's suggestion an idea to preserve the stiffness of the rudder/tiller combination.

The shelf of the rudder on which the tiller rests is made of more durable stuff than the tiller. Gradually the rudder eats into the tiller and the net result is that the tiller sags down onto the deck, scratching the surface as it swings. One of the best ways to control the performance of the boat is positive yet sensitive feel of the rudder by way of the tiller. Keeping the tiller up and stiff achieves this. Alcort has now put a small rubber tip on the end of the tiller to protect the deck, but the real cure lies in gluing two rubber rectangles one eighth inch thick to the shelf.

Tape the tiller where the bridle crosses it. You won't go any faster but the tiller will look prettier and the chafe will be reduced. While on tape, take a few turns at various places on the hiking stick. Some people put a little sand in some varnish and paint it. Others rough sand it. This will help in the frantic grab for the stick after a hard jibe. To come up with a handful of nothing as your sun creamed hand slips off the extension is indeed disappointing.

Alcort has now legalized the use of a tiller extension handle measuring two inches by two inches. The first I saw were really cross pieces and nice jobs of woodwork, but devilish devices for hooking pieces of clothing or life jackets when tacking or jibing.

You must use extension devices because they permit four or five more inches of effective hiking length. As the old rule permitted original equipment only, most of us took the clew outhaul sail set from the boom or the first clip back from the tack on the foot and used it as a hiking stick extension.

We drilled a hole half way into the side of the extension about one half inch back from the end. The nub of the sail set could then be forcibly inserted. We drilled a small hole in the other side of the extension and screwed in the other side of the clip. After gluing and taping we had a good ring from which we could steer while hiking by using the middle finger only.

Now that the extension is legal some people are taking the fun out of invention by making rings of brass pipe with parallel holes on flat sides. They simply bolt through. I will probably go to this method, but the heavier the ring the more powerfully you tend to handle the extension and these break. Holding a handful of hiking stick while sputtering in the water with your boat sailing merrily away teaches you to treat your extension kindly.

You should always check the cap nut on the extension. Peen it over if it looks as though it may be loose at all. Replace extensions regularly; look for signs of wear between the extension and the tiller.

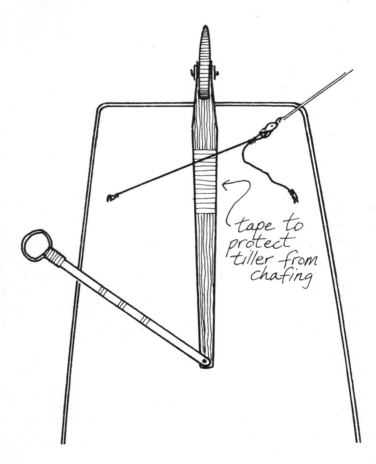

tape to protect tiller from chafing

Some people go through life believing they are sailing straight only to discover to their horror that the tiller straps which connect the rudder to the tiller are slightly bent; the rudder has been at a slight angle all along.

Alcort manufactured some rudders and boards of laminated plywood at one time. I have heard that this material is not good for rudders or boards because the grain is not uniform and therefore you get excessive twist. This may be so, but I have used a rudder of this construction for two years off the rocky beaches at Darien and do not have any significant dents in the edges yet. I would use a board of laminated plywood if I could find one.

Rudders are real drags. Many fine sailors concentrate on steering by the sail, moving the rudder as little as possible. Certainly downwind in light air you will find lots of people who pop their rudder out of the water and steer by the wind and careful positioning of their weight.

For fun you might try to rig a shock cord from the bridle eye straps so that it makes a turn around the tiller and holds the tiller, and therefore the rudder, straight. Then sail with no hands on the tiller and change directions by playing the sail and shifting your weight. You will be amazed that you can not only do it but you will also go fast.

With the use of the "Hoyt Effect" on the port side bridle, increased strain on the plastic covering dictated the use of a small single block to which to affix the sheet. This reduces the friction on the bridle. You might also tie a line from eye strap to eye strap as a sort of double bridle.

# THE HULL

The editors of "One-Design & Offshore Yachtsman" recently commented that the Sunfish is of generally excellent quality and uniformity of manufacture. We would certainly agree, but what can we do to improve on an already good boat?

Rudy Thompson, who has done as much as anyone to upgrade the racing image of the Sunfish, tipped me off about the hull. There are occasionally some bubbles or disfigurements caused in shipping or manufacturing. A hull just a little asymmetrical is going to cause trouble. Inspect the bottom of a new boat very carefully. Make sure the daggerboard slot is lined up with the keelson.

The Long Island Sound Interclub Dinghy sailors are as meticulous about their equipment as any sailing group. Many of them wash the bottoms of their boats in Lux or a similar detergent. They believe there is something slippery in the cleansing agent which makes the boat go faster. As long as there is a low phosphate content, we see no harm in this activity. We recommend it but not because of some magic "go fast" in Lux. A clean bottom is a faster bottom.

There is no doubt that oil spots, weed, road grime, etc., slow down the boat. The evidence is overwhelming. Admittedly a good header or a puff will put a boat further ahead than a clean bottom, but championship racing involves a lot of people who are alert enough to be in the right place at the right time. The winners take the extra care to have competitive equipment.

The deck of the Sunfish can look new for many years if you take care of it. A good fresh water rinse after every use will preserve the luster. White is the most long lasting color. I understand people have had success in getting out scratches with a regular automotive rubbing compound. The best advice is to try to avoid scratches in the first place.

Everyone uses the standard technique of tipping the boat way up to windward on runs in light air. The logic is mainly to reduce wetted surface and perhaps get the sail higher, and certainly to get the rudder out of the water and reduce weather helm. I seemed to have a particularly hard time mastering the technique. To be good at it, you must keep perfectly still. Haven't we all held our breath, locked in silent slow motion combat, not daring to breathe or, heaven forbid, even move, praying for the puff that will squirt us ahead? My trouble was that I would slide slowly and silently off the side of the boat.

My solution is to put a strip of "no slip" sand paper on either side of the cockpit. This is enough to hold me on, but not enough to tear holes in my pants. My first experiments included combining the "no slip" paper and deck lines. The virtually sanded deck certainly ruined four pairs of pants to say nothing of my modesty.

I now of course make deck lines of regular tape. The theory of the deck lines is that you can sight along them and ascertain your relative position in the fleet. As an example — you are on

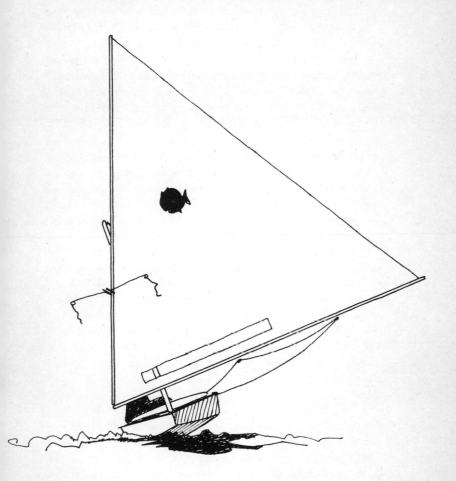

a long course and you are ahead and to leeward of another boat. For one reason or another you want to tack over to his side of the course. Can you cross him? If he is behind the 135 degree line you can theoretically do so. After twice ramming Carl Knight I discovered that one had to take into consideration other factors such as the distance lost in tacking.

There are a number of people, Chuck and Carl Knight included, who do not want to be impeded in their movements about the deck. They won't use "no slip" paper. Particularly in planing conditions where they are moving back and forth on the boat, they want the deck slippery. Do what works best for you.

The aforementioned Rudy Thompson has also introduced me to some daggerboard saving devices which I believe are really vital to peace of mind, to say nothing of boat speed. I have often said that I would not put my mother-in-law in the trunk of this boat and pull her up and down — tempting but humanity would prohibit. Rudy has made the trunk habitable, at least for a daggerboard. He glues thin vinyl strips inside vertically along the fore and aft sections of the trunk. He sands and smooths the edges and fills the crevices with Marine Tex. He files and sands again. This really spoils the Sunfish board, accustomed to splintering at every insertion. Some people fill the crevices with silicone seal. This keeps the edges soft and also doubles as a restraining device for the board.

As noted, some people have glued vinyl strips to the lower aftersides of the trunk to help make a pivoting board. This is illegal.

I have often wondered about the use of "slot rubbers" — a device designed to prohibit the flow of water into the daggerboard trunk. Certainly reduced turbulence is to be desired. The other day we turned the boat over to see how much area is involved. Upwind with the board down, not much, but downwind with the board up — a whole bunch.

Carl Knight came up with an almost perfect device. He glued pieces of foam rubber pipe insulation in the trunk fore and aft. These served as a daggerboard restraining device and satisfied the legal requirements of the class thereby. They also eliminated splinters, scars, etc. Chatter was reduced as the board was snugger. As a slot rubber, however, the insulation was a failure as water came shooting up out of the trunk geyser fashion on planing legs.

If anyone can figure out a legal technique, good on all points of sail, which would reduce the flow of water into the lower trunk, we would appreciate hearing. The rooster tails spewing out of the deckside of the trunk when on a plane are enough to convince us of the need for some type of restraint on the flow of water into the slot.

In short, keep the hull clean, the daggerboard trunk smooth. Rinse the boat in fresh water at every chance. It will reward you for good care.

# FITTINGS—PART ONE

When someone really wants to tee off on the boat they select the rudder fittings as their first target, and probably with reason. In every major regatta where wind has been strong, a rudder has popped up on at least one major contender. Jack Knights at the 1970 World's, John Magenheimer at a couple of his big series, Ward Young at the 1967 Nationals have all had this problem, and hundreds of others have fallen victim.

If Alcort responds to this problem, and they probably will, they will do themselves a great favor. But there will still be lots of older boats — what to do?

We mentioned Bob Johnstone before. He suggested that a small rubber gasket be fitted into the cup at the latch plate. I have done this and found that the resultant lack of rudder wiggle waggle reduced drag enough to make a difference. The rudder seems to stay put since the fit is tighter and there is less vibration. You might even file out the lip of the latch plate cup to make an even more secure fit.

Much of the cause of rudder defection is a bent deck plate. I know some people who will unscrew the plate and press it flat in a vise. I think this part is too malleable. When it bends once it will bend again, and worse. Throw it away, get a new one. Or you might try this idea: When you sail regularly in heavy winds have your deckplate bolted through to the deck as in the picture on page 31.

You might also wire the rudder to the vertical pin if you are in a position to launch regularly from a dock and do not need the pop-up feature of your rudder.

The cockpit of the Sunfish occasionally gets wet. When this happens you are probably getting a leak through the bailer. This leakage is a nuisance but it is easily corrected. Put some silicone seal around the bailer. Also a drop or two of powdered graphite on the bailer at regular intervals is all that is required to keep it in good shape. Rinse it in fresh water regularly too.

One of the items recommended in the Regatta Checklist is a pop rivet tool. The aluminum edging comes off once in a while. After hiking the molding can get loose. This is easily fixed with a drill and pop rivet tool as we will describe. The

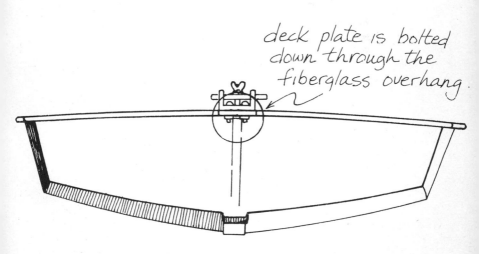

deck plate is bolted down through the fiberglass overhang.

aluminum edging in the cockpit is a relatively new addition to the boat and you might have to make an adjustment to compensate for it as described below.

We still see many pictures taken in the early '60's where the boat is being sailed like a bucking bronco — the sheet leading directly to the sailors' hands with no device to flatten the sail or aid in sheeting. Alcort introduced the open fairlead or "hook" and a welcome addition it was. If you do not use the center jam swivel cleat, you must use the "hook".

If you have the least bit of trouble in getting the sheet under the hook, drop the fairlead down ¼ to ½ inch. Then the hook will be below the edging and your troubles will be over.

The other way to compensate for the edging is to bring the hook out by use of a shim. To border on legality, some have cut out a piece of sail set and inserted it between the lip of the cockpit and the hook.

Alcort does not plan for racing in extreme conditions. Indeed it is not often that you race with a cockpit full of water, but occasionally you do. If you think you might, put silicone seal around the top of the cockpit where it meets the deck.

Also, when you have purchased a new hull you now have a nice cubby hole into which you can stuff various things — sponges, gloves, etc. The best thing to put in the recess area is a pair of underinflated medium sized beach balls. Air is lighter than water and the space these balls take up displaces a much heavier amount of water should you be sailing in extreme conditions. Very clever these Sunfishers — thinking all the time. Some rudder pins do not fit the deck plate. A little filing at the hinge will take care of that problem. Don't peen over the top of the vertical pin. The wing nut almost never comes off and you do need the flexibility.

Dr. Bill Kennedy, Fish Champ from the Gulf Coast, upon his first look at the Sunfish recommended that the latch plate be rounded and smoothed. I don't believe you can legally fair this plate, but I do know you can sand it to the texture of a baby's skin. You should.

Since there are no restrictions on the type of finishes used on the bottom or the degree of smoothness, you may and should sand the bailer. The bailer is more dangerous than even the rough texture would imply however. When you take it off to sand make sure you put it back in line. It has a reasonably streamlined shape, make use of it.

When you put it back, make sure you put some silicone seal around it. The bailer is a most subversive weed catcher. You never think of this as the area causing you to slow down drastically. You can check the board and rudder but what can you do about weed streaming from the bailer anyway — other than just wait?

If you wish, remove the rubber gasket from the bottom of the bailer and put it on the cockpit side of the seal between the bailer and the deck so there is no chance of weed catching. Back up on deck you should make sure water cannot seep into the bridle, causing a break at some critical point in a regatta. I used to tape over each end but I understand that some people melt the ends, making the tube airtight.

Some people put inspection ports into the hull so they can check for water and easily bail. It is a great idea which we heartily recommend. Only do so when you suspect leaks, however; there is no sense in surgery unless it is called for. A Holt-Allen port is good; I use a clear plastic one from Nicro. Install them on the aft portion of the deck, between the bridle eye straps.

# FITTINGS—PART TWO

The subject of jam cleats is one that AMF—Alcort's Bruce Connolly could write a book about. For years people had been badgering him to permit some form of jam cleat. Finally in 1968 he relented. A mainsheet jam or cam action cleat was legalized. In 1971 the rule was extended to include more than one mainsheet cleat if desired.

Alcort's objection to jam cleats was that not every boat would have one, thus spoiling the one-design nature of the class. They further felt that jam cleats were rather expensive and if they were allowed the flood gates would be opened to more expensive additions to the boat. One of the charms of the Sunfish is its relatively low price; Alcort wanted to keep it that way.

I agree with this logic but the jam cleat makes life so simple that the device is almost a necessity. The real objection to the jam cleat should have been that it is dangerous when not properly used. The center swivel variety tends to stick at just the wrong moment, usually on a jibe or a tack, and over you go. New sailors should proceed with caution when considering jam cleats. I would not prescribe one for my kids.

There are a number of types of jam cleats and there does not seem to be agreement on the best. It probably is a matter of taste and what you have become accustomed to. Bill King, one of the finest gentlemen and competitors in the sport, used my rig the other day. He hated it. He uses the center swivel cleat while I usually use two clam cleats mounted to the side decks.

From my standpoint any device which uses a closed fairlead such as the center swivel jam, restricts your ability to sheet in quickly. I think it is vital to be able to reach out and grab a lot of sheet at one time. Dinghy starting many times involves a slow luffing along the line and then a rapid trimming of the sails only seconds before the start with many other boats doing the same thing in very close proximity.

I spent many hours tinkering with other types. First I used a set of cam cleats similar to those used on the side decks of the Finn. I found that to insure that the sheet was in place I had to come in from hiking and press the sheet down. The sheet was coming up from the cockpit at such an angle that it was difficult to lay it in flat in the cleat. Then I put a half inch shim under the cleats and it was easier to secure the mainsheet. I still had trouble with this rig, however. Sand played havoc with the gears and I never seemed to get the spring tension right.

Jack Evans, one of the more imaginative Sunfish sailors, has found an Italian cam cleat which sits about two inches off its base. This looks as though it would be a good one and also might serve as a hand hold.

I finally found what was for me the right answer. I use two clam cleats. This is a plastic encased claw with nice wide jaws into which I can drop the sheet blindfolded. The cleat has no moveable parts for me to foul and it is tall enough so that it

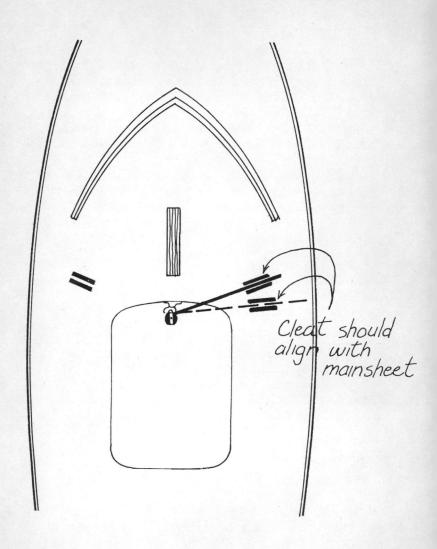

Cleat should align with mainsheet

does not require a shim. I position the cleats so that they are opposite each other with the inboard end just at that section of the deck where a bolt can be used and fastened to the underside of the lip. They angle away from the cockpit to the same degree as the sheet leading from the hook. The position is a matter of taste; Chuck has his cleats perpendicular to the cockpit.

The clam cleat is a great asset. It is a third hand. I find I use it before a major move in order to get organized. I will also confess to using it when I am bushed going upwind in a breeze — but only for a moment you understand. Most of us don't really use a cleat much in a heavy breeze; you have to adjust the sail so much according to puffs and sea conditions that you cannot afford to leave the sheet cleated.

At the 1970 World's I put a standard free running block on the deck positioned just where the center jam is normally located. I did this because the courses were over six miles in length with three full beats. I reasoned that with starting lines a quarter mile long, I could find a hole someplace where sheet-ing in and out would not be as critical. The time saved in tacking with a block would be significant as would the ability to adjust more easily to big seas. I still believe this would have been a good device, but Larry Pratt, Sales Manager of Alcort, who had the unenviable task of enforcing the rules against a bunch of Henry Ford/Rube Goldbergs, outlawed me. Chuck independently arrived at the same conclusion as I, but his rig was upheld. Carl Knight went a step or so further. He showed up with a console. John Dane has a console in his Soling — Carl has a console in his Sunfish. Some called it a rolltop desk. It contained a pencil holder, chart holder, notebook, and stop watch holder. It was on a rotating piece of mahogany and had a block, a jam cleat and a compass. His unit was disallowed. There is just no hope for young Edisons in this class.

Chuck, however, installed a Lewmar ratchet block. This block served the same purpose as mine but it also had a cam action jam cleat which made it legal. I feel that this was

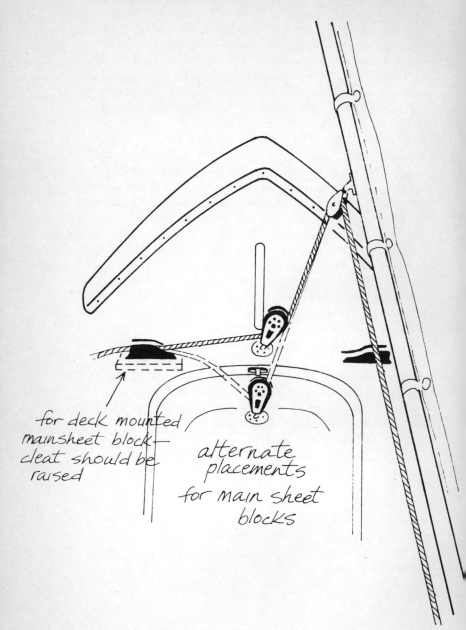

for deck mounted
mainsheet block—
cleat should be
raised

alternate
placements
for main sheet
blocks

stretching the rules a bit but since it was allowed you can't argue. One of the moments I will always cherish was the day Jeorg Bruder came out to sail with us in practice on Cowpet Bay. Chuck boomed out on his weather quarter, using the ratchet. Jeorg ducked, thinking some Twelve Meter was bearing down on him. The Harken ratchet has become the most popular.

In light air on relatively short courses, I still believe in the freedom of the simple clam cleats. On long Olympic type courses in a heavy sea and breeze, I think a combination ratchet plus clam cleats is desirable. Once you get used to a rig it is difficult to change, so start with the one which suits the conditions you most often will sail in.

# FITTINGS—PART THREE

Just forward of the jam cleats is an area which is too often overlooked: the splashboard which is secured by 12 bolts. Gradually these small holes develop leaks. Surround the board with silicone seal. Alcort may be responsive to the pleas of their overseas distributors and change the splashboard as the part is too flexible for shipping and frequently gets damaged.

The splashboard is also used by some sailors as a vang. They have filed away the outer lower ends of the board. They hook the sheet underneath on a reach. This is probably illegal as it constitutes an alteration of the boat.

AMF—Alcort replaced the old bullet shaped main halyard cleat with an adequate but less accommodating one. The purchase you got with the old one was better and quicker.

Garry Hoyt made the comment recently that for $10 worth of fittings the boat could be substantially improved. I assume he was talking about blocks but probably not the main halyard block. We have never heard this block maligned. Bob Bowles cuts the side of his deck block. He ties his halyard and sheet together to avert catastrophe in case he drops the sheet. By having the deck block open he can unrig more easily.

The halyard itself is cotton. The halyard shrinks. Even braided Dacron shrinks. You are permitted 24 feet of halyard. I cheat by using 24 feet of spun polyester. This material looks like cotton but it does not shrink. How many times between races have you had to undo your halyard and rehoist the sail because the halyard has stretched? What stretches will shrink and ultimately you will end up with 22 or so feet and this will cost you in a light air race as will be described on page 63. If you do use polyester halyards make sure you burn the ends. Also do not use braided polyester. It slips up the gaff and your rig gets so low you cannot get under the boom when you tack. The best way to insure no slippage up the gaff is to tie the halyard to a piece of no slip paper glued to the spar.

Bruce Connolly is the one who gets credit for responding to the pleas of us older gentlemen to permit Dacron sheets. I think this one move created a great many sales and retained a lot of old customers. Cotton is a great fiber but cotton sheets tear up your hands. Soft braided filament Dacron sheets are easier on us. We suggest you serve the ends of the sheet too as the sheet tends to ravel into itself. I now use a 3/8-inch Marlowe spun polyester sheet; ¼-inch in light air.

Skip Cook used to mark the sheet according to various conditions of breeze. This has real merit as long as you clip the bridle at the same point all the time, making sheet length constant. Once you get in the groove, make a mark on the sheet so that the next time you sail in those conditions you can put it into automatic pilot and away you go. I have read that people sew a black thread into the sheet to serve as a control point. This is meticulousness above and beyond the call — but I bet the people who do it are either winners or have more fun at the game.

The last area to be covered in the discussion of the sheet is just that. Please tie a knot in the end of it after passing it through the blocks on the boom.

My wife, Brownie, stood in the top 10 at the Light Corinthians in 1970 — and in a 15 knot breeze came the jibing mark and she lost the sheet. It ran through the blocks with no knot to encumber it. End of Light Corinthians. Guess whose husband had rigged the boat and had forgotten to tie the knot?

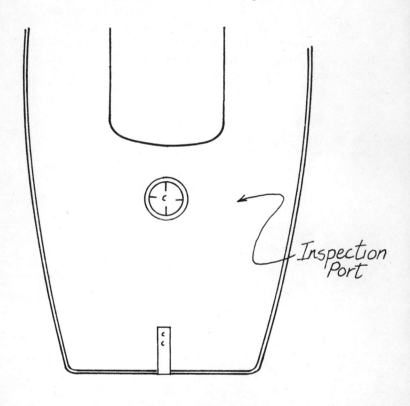

Inspection Port

# FITTINGS—PART FOUR

For many years I did not use a tell tale. And for all those years I dogged it in the lower half of the fleet in light air races. I believe that when I changed to a good tell tale system my performance improved at the same time.

You must have both a masthead fly and a lower indicator. If you don't have both you are wrong. You are losing an opportunity to increase your speed.

Everyone has his own tell tale system. Bob Bowles uses the Telo feathers. They get caked with salt, so if you use them make sure your wife or girl friend washes them out every evening. When they get wet, they don't perform too well. In light air, however, they appear to be very sensitive. They can be dried on the air conditioner of a car in two hours. In the rain, you should use magnetic recording tape — impervious to water.

Bob Bushnell, long an advocate of the "wind on your cheek" school, now uses a bullet shaped wind vane on the bow. Will White uses, as do the Finn boys, a number 10 wire with nylon yarn. He tapes the wire to the gaff. The DuPont people will be pleased to know that nylon fabric is one of the favorite tell tales. A piece of nylon stocking is an excellent fly.

I like my tell tale the best. It is a combination of ideas from Messers. Bowles, White and Ding Schoonmaker. I take an electrical clamp to which I attach pieces of number 10 wire 18 inches long on either side. I use red Orlon yarn. Nylon is o.k. too! Wool takes too long to dry. The picture of my rig is on the next page.

In big breezes tell tales lose some of their importance but not completely. When you are sailing in big seas the apparent wind changes from trough to crest; only with a masthead fly can you really correct the set of your sail. And in light stuff it really pays.

I remember one of the really horrible days of sailing in 1970. The Brookhaven Bath Bottle and Boating Society put on one of the most memorable regattas of the year. Saturday saw an awful Northwester, full of holes, and 180 degree shifts. The wind was just itching to back to the Southwest. The near reach to the finish was a study of frustration. Bryce Suydam was just ahead of me and to starboard on my weather bow. Fifty yards to the finish. He had his masthead fly; I did not. All of a sudden his fly did a 180. I let my sail out, ran up behind him, took his air, and ghosted across, just ahead of the onrushing pack. So be kind to your competitors, use a masthead fly.

One more thing about my electrical clamp. If someone hits you and bends the wire it is easy to go up, take the clamp off, fix the wire and put the clamp back up. With the taped kind you are usually done for if the wire is bent. Bob Bowles should have patented the idea.

I used to panic when I lost my tell tale. I still don't like to sail without it, but I find that when push comes to shove I sail

exclusively by the luff of the sail and I can get along. When
you get into a round robin series where you change boats, you
will have to get used to sailing with different tell tales and
sometimes with no indicator at all. You should practice for
this by sailing for fun with no fly. But in an important series
you must use the tell tale. You can pick up lifts on windward
legs much more readily.

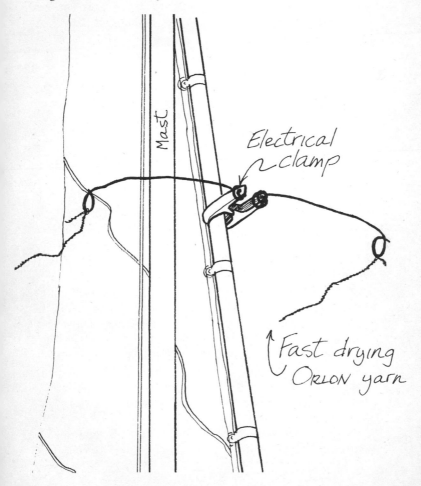

## TUNING–SAILS

This last segment of the tuning portion is for us the most nebulous of all — sails. Everyone tells us this is the motor of the boat. And yet Sunfish sails which have curled leeches, look like corrugated washboards or have twisted peaks seem to do well in the hands of the better sailors. The moral in this is that the sail in the Sunfish is not nearly as important as the skipper who can adjust to the vagaries of the wind.

Don't misunderstand, you should strive to get your sail to be the best possible: free of hard spots, no sewing imperfections, a nice firm leech, full draft about 40% aft, no flutter, no twist at the peak or the foot. When you get this you have got the ultimate — you may have had to send it back to Ratsey for recutting which is perfectly proper; you may not send it to other sailmakers, however. Even so we contend that there are very narrow differences between the best and the worst of the Ratsey sails.

First, rig your sail right. Alcort positions the gooseneck
21½ inches aft of the tack on a black band. The spot is there
because of the suggested location of the halyard on the spar. If
you tie the halyard where we suggest you will have a different
looking sail plan than you see in Alcort publicity pictures.
Alcort suggests a high sail probably because they don't want to
have new sailors get a knock on the noggin when they tack. As
long as you want to race and are mindful of the low boom, rig

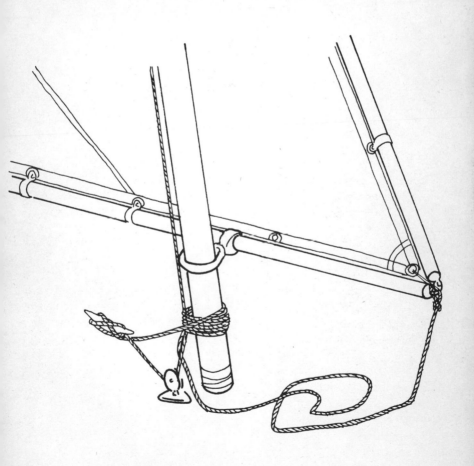

the halyard nine to 9½ grommets up from the tack. Move the gooseneck back one or two inches. There is little doubt that the resultant lower sail plan is better for speed, particularly in a breeze.

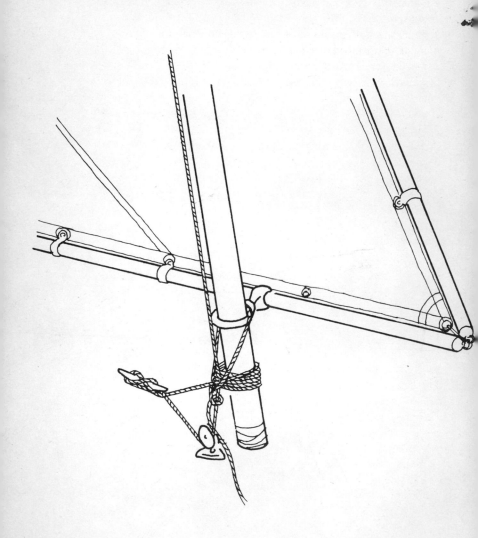

If you weigh less than 160 pounds fully clothed you can afford to put the halyard up to the 10th grommet in a breeze of 15 knots and up. And even move the gooseneck back to 24 inches from the tack. Put a line around the ninth grommet so that the mast on port tack doesn't bind the sail set and create a hard spot.

Tape the gooseneck screw. I never had a sail in which I didn't develop tiny holes at the gooseneck area until I started taping the screw. Also watch how you furl the sail; sometimes it pinches between the spars and the friction creates small holes.

When you hoist the sail, pulling the halyard through the block, cleat the line securely and then take a couple of lashes around the mast, drawing the halyard around it as in the picture, left. There is no sense in having the halyard a couple of inches away from the mast creating a separate drag. Take advantage of every opportunity to reduce wind resistance.

After lashing the halyard to the mast you can do other things with it as well. If there is a big breeze you can bring it over the goose neck as in the picture, left, and pull it down hard. This serves as a sort of vang, flattening the sail. You can also bring the halyard out on the boom as in the picture on the next page. This is the type of vang favored by most sailors.

In light air tie the end of the halyard to the interlocking eyebolts. When you are going downwind in light air and you try to tip the boat up to windward frequently there is not enough breeze to keep the sails full and then the boat inadvertently jibes. By pulling on the halyard from the windward side you can keep the sail full and drawing. This contraption is known as a J.C. Strap after its inventor John Christianson.

Some people tie the gaff to the mast. This is probably illegal but it does reduce the possibility of the halyard slipping or coming undone.

In the days of the Florida midwinters, Bob Bowles and I would slug up the weather leg and arrive in good shape at the first mark after surviving the short ugly steep seas of Biscayne

Bay. That body of water is pernicious; it literally rattles the bones. In any event, very shortly after turning to the reaching leg, zip — there would go young Doug Brown planing by. I wasn't disturbed but Bob was and is an off wind master and he couldn't believe what was happening to him.

Bob studied Doug's sail and sure enough there was a difference. Doug had a standard sail, but that year the standard had been changed without our knowledge. More draft had been

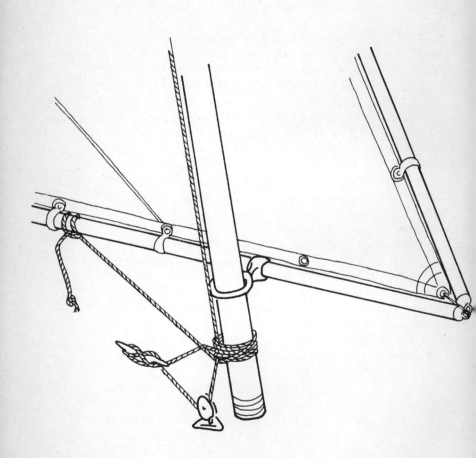

added. At the Brookhaven regatta in 1970 all sails were measured, probably to legislate against some people who had repairs done by local sailmakers and a little piece added here and there in the right place.

My sail measured 84.43 square feet. New sails out of the bag were as much as 88 square feet. The old 75 square feet days, if they ever existed, were over. All sails with a Ratsey and Lapthorn white signature patch are old and small unless they have an S or SS imprinted over the Ratsey name. We see Jim Carson, top New Jersey Lightning skipper, sailing perfect tactical races in Sunfish and losing. He has an old white patch sail. Any red patch sail is a new better sail. Don't believe people who claim there is a real difference in the area of the new sails. The shapes may be different from tuning and usage but the areas are comparable. I believe the best Ratsey sails to date have an L designator on the patch.

At Darien we hold our Bermuda Crown series. This is a 10 boat round robin event. The average position of the winning skipper this year was 3.3 — the last place sailor averaged 7.9. The average finishing position of the leading boat was 4.4 and the tail ender was 6.8. No super boats — the best averaged worse than fourth and there were no dogs — the worst averaged better than seventh. The difference in the performance of the boats is extremely narrow as you can see. We conclude that Sunfish reasonably well tuned and rigged are competitive with each other.

Methods of rigging the sail itself differ but most of us now subscribe to the Bowles/Knight method. They developed very loose rigs, restraining the clew outhaul at zero tension. The sail set which under natural rigging would fall at the forward sheet block on the boom is left either undone or drawn forward of the block. The sail set just aft of the tack is removed. Now this is a loose footed sail. It also creates a great deal of draft forward.

Make no mistake, this loose rig is not universally used. Garry Hoyt has his sail further out on the spars as does Carl

Knight, in a breeze. We think the shape of the sail is improved by loose rigging, and although scallops form along the edges the number of hard spots would be reduced in the most critical areas of sail power, and most important, the leech stays firm. Pull the foot of the sail out to the point of a firm leech in light air, and a non-cupped leech in a breeze.

In the days of smaller sails, many people used lace lines. This was in an attempt to loose foot the sail, and resulted in the Alcort rule on the sail not being more than two inches from the spar. Another reason for lacing the grommets is to change the draft in the sail for various reasons. Adjustable outhauls, however, are illegal. Notice on pages 66-67 how much draft is developed in this sail on a dead run. The sail is extremely loose footed.

Bill King has a nifty use for the lace line. He reeves his through the tack and back behind the gooseneck. He then undoes the gooseneck and it is able to slide along, restrained by the lace line. I prefer to stay simple and use sail sets only. If you use lace line I suggest you use Dacron or Nylon as cotton tends to shrink and form uneven tensions on the foot, creating hard spots.

Most of us pull the sail up taut. If hard spots form or the peak twists excessively, loosen the outhaul and you will free the sail somewhat.

Rudy Thompson introduced most of the class to one of the best developments to come along in years! The long rectangular window. Most of us were too unimaginative to take advantage of the 1x2 foot rectangular window previously authorized. All we could see was the almost box like windows that a few people had and most discarded.

Rudy put a four inch window in his sail, stretching from the tack aft about six feet. This 288 square inch window has the same area as the old one but is a lot more useful. You can see dead downwind; you can more easily judge your position relative to another boat. When you are to weather of someone right after the start you don't have to move unnecessarily to get your position; now you can watch all the way.

Some port tackers judge that if they can see a starboard tacker in their window they have to tack; if they cannot they can continue on their course assuming the starboard boat cannot reach them. Don't believe it.

You should rinse your sail in fresh water after every use in salt water. Don't iron your sail. If you are going to store the sail let it hang loose, releasing luff tension in particular. You should have a sail bag in which to carry your sail and spars. The sail stays cleaner and there is less chance of developing holes. Don't leave your sheet on the spars with the sail. Sheets pick up sand and sand abrades sails badly. Don't wind your halyard around the sail. Leave the sail loosely furled and slide it into the spar bag. Take care of your sail, it will reward you.

# STARTS

It's all over now but the sailing. Tuning, exercising, rigging, the hours of meticulous preparation are through. We promise you that if you have followed all of the steps we have recommended you are ready for any World's.

The lines are usually excellent at major events. Systems are in accordance with NAYRU regulations. What techniques will we use to get out of the box, in clear air and moving to the favored side of the course? (And remember, winds shift, lines don't always stay perfect.)

Jeorg Bruder taught most of us a lesson at the '70 World's. After the first race he realized the need to get clear air right at the start. Thereafter he would start high of the line and with a few seconds to go would boom down, dipping into a hole and moving at the gun. Jeorg never had a problem upwind when he had one of those starts. There is no doubt that on big lines in huge fleets this method is successful. If you don't get caught over the line. Living life in this manner is for the hardy. Garry Hoyt did not resort to this at the '70 World's, which he won, but at the '70 Caribbean Championships he was hustling at the leeward end right on the line. So, the first recommendation on starts is get clear air. If you don't choose to achieve it by dipping or by getting the one perfect start at the favored end, get it by going a quarter way down the line from the favored side, or get it at the weather end by being the second boat past the committee boat and tacking over to the starboard side of the course immediately.

However, many races are decided today by starts governed by the locally enforced five minute rule or the IYRU one minute rule, applicable after a general recall. The five minute rule proved Jeorg Bruder's undoing at the '70 World's. What now, you dippers?

The law now gives a lot more power to the leeward yacht prior to the start. Many people find the standard technique of luffing weather yachts until the start and then diving into the hole they have carved to leeward to be even more potent under the 1969 rules. Most winning starters go with way on. What results when you stall out the boat to weather is that you stall yourself and some enterprising soul darts through to leeward with a full rap on and you are wallowing in his back-wind.

So, my advice: A minute or so before the start be up to weather of the lay line at the favored end if it is to starboard. Beware of the boat approaching to leeward; if you see one and the time till the start is still adequate, bear down and discourage him from going to leeward of you. Usually he will luff up to weather of you. As long as his bow does not get ahead of yours you can usually forget him.

Now come up, keep up. If you have any more boats trying to come through to leeward, fake going down. By now enough Barrett starters have filled in below you that any boat trying to go through you to leeward has too much fiberglass ahead; they will luff up. Keep up, keep up. Now a few seconds before the start, drive, bear down on a leeward boat if you are bow to bow, luff up if not, sheet in, go!

But don't go before the gun. Use a stopwatch. Dinghy starts today at well organized clubs have two or three minute sequences with nice loudly hailed countdowns. Don't get used to this luxury. Use a watch. Carl Knight leaves nothing to chance in this regard; he uses two watches.

Normally NAYRU starting rules apply. My way of remembering the sequence which is a white flag at 10 minutes, blue flag at five and red at the start, with white and blue going down 30 seconds before the next flag is raised, is We /Better/ Race — White/ Blue/Red.

In the Caribbean Championships of 1970, Tito Casales ran a tight Race Committee. He started on time. When the line is downwind from the beach you cannot hear the gun sometimes. Now that is when experience pays. Look at the signal on the Race Committee launch. It's Blue — get to the line. If it is still up that means you have at least thirty seconds. I have seen two regattas blown on just this mistake. The real moral, of course, is get out early.

When I am out early I find a friend, usually Chuck. We start at opposite ends of the line on converging courses. Which end is favored? We continue on to the lay line for the mark, tack and converge again. Which side of the course was favored? Is there a drifting anchor line? Is there a current? Was the favored side of the course caused by a permanent condition or was it an oscillating wind? Then I sail to the reaching mark, I sight down from mark to mark to make sure I have the proper bearing. Once in a while I am ahead and I have gone in the wrong direction all too often.

Now I am back to the line. Incidentally, if the waves are so huge that you cannot see the marks at a distance, you had better get a good fix with a land point beforehand. I check the line again. Still one end favored? In a really oscillating wind I time the shifts; usually there is a pattern.

I determine the weather end lay line. I do it again. If I am wearing sweatshirts, I go over and get them wet. I sponge out the cockpit. I check the lines and the fittings. I'm nervous just writing about it. I fasten down the wing nut. I check for weed, pull up the board, brush off the rudder. One or two more fast sails to remember speed and then at about seven or eight minutes to go I sit down in the cockpit and relax and watch. What is Garry doing? Where are the leaders concentrating? I watch for the five minute signal, check my watch. I get up, sail around, I want to get used to speed again. Line still the same? Cockpit dry? Am I going for a port tack? If so I begin to go to that end of the line. If not I go up to the line about halfway and loaf along. I get on the line regardless of wind, but it is dramatically important in light air or against a foul current. Stay up on the bloody line!

One-and-a-half minutes — remember if seas are huge allow extra time for slow tacking. Turn, go toward the fleet. The first race syndrome may be on them all; they may be line shy. Tack to weather of a likely weaker opponent, to leeward of a stronger one. Really most important. 30 seconds. Come up just over that lay line — tell those weather boats there won't be any room. Keep moving. Don't get caught on the line with a perfect position and no speed. Keep the leeward boat well down. Last second look at the watch, sheet in and drive ———gun!

There are several other starting techniques to consider. We mentioned "Barrett starters" before. Basically, this is the crowd who approach the line on port tack and flip in front of an oncoming starboard boat. Usually this is achieved with success at the port end. It should be timed so that the tack is completed and the boat is just above the lay line to the pin with enough time remaining to hit the line with the gun.

The counter offense against the Barrett start by the starboard boat is a subtle alteration of course so that the port tack boat comes about below the lay line and cannot fetch the pin when he tacks and makes his run for it. I hold that there is no proper course before the start and that as long as the provisions of Rule 34 are satisfied you can alter course so that the port boat cannot risk tacking. The rights of the close hauled port boat under Rule 34 change only when his sails go past head to wind so he won't risk tacking too close.

Most new sailors would be well advised to go halfway down the line and find clear air rather than attack the favored end. You will find that the 20 or 30 yards you give up will be regained by the fact that you have free air. Be sure to be on

the line, however. Many new sailors think they are on the line but are really several boat lengths below.

Finally there will come the day when you get the perfect start at one end or another — and the wind will shift. Have the guts to take the sterns of those on the favored side. Absorb your 50 yard loss quickly; it becomes hundreds of yards if you

don't get over to the correct side of the course in a real hurry. Remember that all those sterns you are taking are headed in the wrong direction so that when you flip back over you are being lifted up on their quarter. Regattas are won on making the fewest errors! The ability to recognize an error and rectify it promptly is what wins! In an oscillating wind, however, if it lifts behind you, hang on, it will come back.

The sequence on pages 74 through 79 tells the story graphically.

Notice that 199 and 102 are jockeying for the perfect leeward start, but they may have lost sight of the committee boat and may be too far down the line from the pin. The tide is against them.

Number 138 begins to gain speed and sail over the slowly

luffing boats ahead of him, dipping down into a hole just before the start. He may be over but there are a number of red and white sails to weather of him and it is not possible to make a really accurate determination; this is a really good example of a "Bruder" start.

All three yachts are being sailed flat but number 199 recog-

nizes at once that he is being backwinded and drives off to leeward to get clear air. Number 102 spots the shift behind him and makes up his mind to take a number of sterns. Number 102 finished 7th in the race. Number 138 would not give up his clear air and ultimately rounded the weather mark 60th.

# TO WEATHER

You're off. Clear air. Can't miss — but you can. Now comes another key point. Bob Bushnell used to clean up in this class. His technique was based on extreme effort, 100% for five minutes. He is in such good shape at that time, he can look around and sail an intelligent rather than a physical race. The moral: 100% concentration for 60 seconds — get speed, speed, speed. But then look. Do you want to get over to port?

The best sailors at Darien sometimes don't win the starts but in short order they are on their way to the favored side in clear air. Their speed takes care of the rest. If you are trapped, get out of there.

My son, Sam, started at Darien one day on a line just slightly port end favored. He had the weather start because most of the hot shots felt the port side of the course was where they wanted to be, but one thing he knew; and it is one thing no more than 10% of any fleet either knows or responds to. All those boats to leeward whose bows are slightly ahead of yours or even directly even are giving you some degree of backwind. If you start to weather on a good line, unless your bow is slightly ahead or there is some really compelling reason to get to the port side of the course, tack out of there.

Sam tacked, cleared a couple of late starters, got gradually headed and in spite of his father suggesting that he tack on the first glimpse of the header he held on until deep enough to come about and lay the weather mark. Sam won his first Darien race at age 14. He will win more.

So the first moral to weather is to get out of the parade. Take a stern or two, don't fight that leeward boat slightly ahead of you unless he is really a less experienced sailor. Tack, clear your air. Clear air is the name of the game.

Sunfish races are usually very short. Tidal current or local shifts are certainly a factor, but the wind at the time is the real key. Sail on the wind; don't sail to spots.

Sure, Rob Brooke, 20 boats behind on the reaching leg at Chelsea on the Hudson, went dead downwind along the shore holding out of the current long enough to beam reach across the fleet to beat the other boats who had held a broad reaching course to the mark.

Yes, holding to the east on a southerly at Darien usually pays in order to duck the current and maybe to pick up a land breeze. But time after time, tacking on headers, following the wind, is what pays. Go on the header. As you get in Chuck's class sometimes you can violate the rule, but usually sail on the course which is the more direct one for the mark.

How often, when we are behind, we will go off on a course on the wrong tack just to do something different in fervent hopes of catching a lucky shift. The good sailor may tack to clear his air, but he will come back, following the leader on the right course, knowing that everybody makes a mistake in a sailboat race, and the leader's time will come.

One thing has helped me in my upwind performance. For years I sailed in the ignominy of being the real tailender in gentle breezes. The cheerful Falstaffian loser. No more.

Secret number one: Lose weight. This has already been covered, of course. If you weigh 170 or less you can win in any conditions except the five to 10 knot days in a chop when the kids will tear you up. There is just no way you can go as fast as the good sailor who weighs 30 or 40 pounds less in these conditions.

In light airs I found that concentration on the sail and tacking smoothly have been important. I think you can even cleat the sheet in light flat sea days, reducing the possibility of overtrimming. In a chop you must hold the sheet in your hand adjusting the sail for the changes in apparent wind due to the waves.

Many people, Chuck included, believe in roll tacking. He teaches this method in his classes. Essentially he dips to windward before coming about, rolling the boat over. I prefer to keep the boat flat. I weigh more and feel I must move less. My rather flat tack is for light air only.

Now, upwind in a breeze. You are physically trained. You should beat seven out of 10 people in the class just because of strength. How does Garry get that little extra? First, the famous Hoyt Effect. Garry reasons that in 20 knot breezes he cannot hold the boat as flat as he would like so he simply unsnaps the sheet and moves it to the port bridle. It then looks like the picture on the next page.

Thus on starboard he creates a traveller effect — lowering the boom, moving it outboard, flattening the sail and making the boat easier to sail level. Port tack does not have as much power as starboard in the Sunfish because of the lateen rig, so there is no need to have the sheet adjust over to the starboard bridle on that tack.

Remember that the snap has a tendency to come unhooked so it is a good idea to tie a bowline in it, passing around the bridle. You may tape the snap.

Garry's technique has been overdone. It reduces pointing ability. The only conditions in which it is really effective are

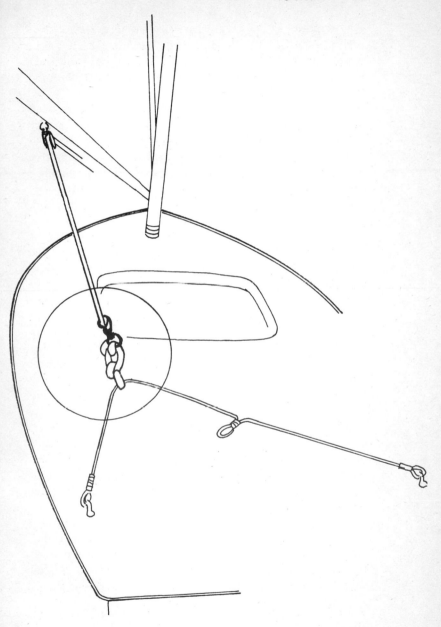

the overpowering ones. I can recall tacking to weather of Ken Klein in the '70 World's and being elated that I ate out to weather of him. All of a sudden, Ken, who used the Hoyt Effect, was footing off to leeward, holding the boat level and there he was, tacking and crossing my bow on port.

Now, regardless of gimmicks there is only one way to go upwind — flat. The Sunfish must be sailed level. Only in very light airs may you permit the boat to heel in either direction and that is only to improve the sail shape and should not be done in flat seas. My friend and son, Sam, will get increasingly tired of the cry from his father "sit forward". You should really steer this boat from the centerboard trunk. Sit forward. Sail it flat.

The main error most of us make in going to weather is holding the boat too high on the wind. Pinching is a sin. The boat wants to sail free. Particularly if you are sailing in a sea, don't pinch. My major mistake in sailing today is the naive belief that I can physically horse the boat upwind higher than anybody. All I achieve is leeway and the footer keeps the boat level, makes more forward yards and ends up ahead. Even in 10-knot breezes I am learning not to muscle the boat higher when a puff comes. I let out the sheet enough to keep the boat flat, rather than feathering up in the puff. Then I gradually pull in the sheet and sail up through the puff, the key being to keep the boat balanced flat.

When sailing in a seaway, sail up on the face of the wave, drive off the back and then up the next front. In essence sail a scalloped course keeping the boat driving.

When the breezes are really heavy, I have had superior results with raising the board a few inches, letting the sheet out and footing off.

We have mentioned tell tales before. Again, keep your eye on the fly. Most of us don't sense lifts as quickly as we should. The tell tales indicate lifts much more promptly than most of us mortals can recognize one. A header is more easily seen by the fact that the sail begins to shiver, but the lift is tougher.

While on your way upwind, watch out for wind interference. If someone comes across on port, encourage him to pass you, not tack below and give you backwind. If someone tacks on your wind, tack away immediately. Don't wait.

Don't play lay lines. You almost can never win by going out to the lay line early in the windward leg. Why? If a lifting shift occurs you have overstood. If a heading shift appears you have to tack again and the boats on the opposite tack are now coming across being lifted. If you are behind, the boats will

**Plans for Hiking Bench constructed of 2x10 and 2x4 timbers**

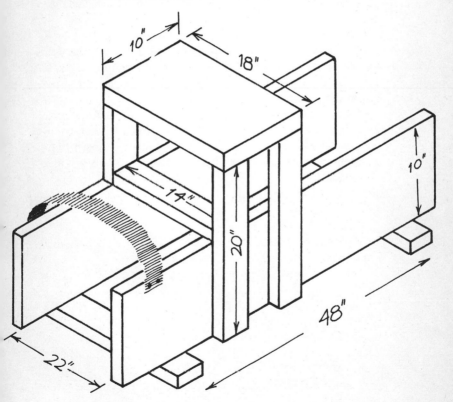

come in and tack on your air as people tend to gradually overstand the closer they get to the mark for fear of having someone else tack on their air. Only in very steady breezes can you afford to go to the lay line early. Usually you should approach a mark on port. You have clearer air. You can tack under an overstander or on top of an understander. Only with a long line of starboard boats are you in trouble and even then you can usually dart under a stern, proceed a length or two and then boom out on their quarters as they pinch for the mark.

Finally, don't overlook concentration, confidence and competitiveness. If you concentrate on the sail or tell tale and have the confidence that your boat is well tuned, you should stay right in there. What happens to me when I am sailing in Bruder/Hoyt company is that I am not awfully sure I can hold them boat for boat, even if I have tactical superiority. I split with them looking over my shoulder and gradually, after tacking on the shifts, they have worn me down.

There is no reason for this attitude. If I can sail 20 or 30 yards equally with them, I should be able to sail a whole course with them. I think this spirit should pervade everybody; the lack of it, the lack of confidence, competitiveness and then concentration when near a class hot shot, is far more damaging than a slow boat.

# REACHING

If any of you wonders why the kids flock to Hawaii in quest of good surf, I can now answer the question. Sailing a Sunfish on the literally downhill reach at Puerto Azul, site of the '71 World's, was one of the most exhilarating sports activities I have ever experienced.

Even though these are extreme conditions, there are some basic principles to be learned all the same. This is the point of sail where the most yardage is to be gained or lost. Tactics are important as is a knowledge of the rules, but probably the technique of making the boat go fast is more important. Let's sail a typical reach, assuming you are entering it from a weather mark.

First, you must plan the reach as you are approaching the windward mark. If you are behind and there is a cluster of boats ahead, plan to bear off immediately upon rounding the mark to sail low on the leg. It's a good bet that boats in a group will gradually go high of the direct line to the next mark. This is the cardinal sin of this point of sail. Stay low.

Also if you do happen to have someone right on your tail, bear off immediately upon rounding the weather mark before he reaches it; discourage him from going off. Remember once you are both on the same leg of the course, Rule 39 prohibits you from bearing off if a boat within three lengths is steering a course to pass you to leeward; you bear off first, before he rounds the mark, and this keeps him high.

How many times have I rounded, pulled up the board, bailed a couple of times, adjusted the sheets and settled into the reach only to find someone has come from astern, taken my wind and pulled over me? Your first job when rounding the mark is to get on a plane; do your housekeeping later.

If you can quickly get on a plane, the course be damned. Naturally, if you can you should bear off when you have speed and come up when you are slowing; but planing gains so much yardage over other boats not on one that you can afford to carry the plane almost to where it takes you and then come back.

How do you get on the plane? Rule 60 has never been invoked in my years of sailing; at least in planing conditions. Therefore, I believe you can ooch, which is bouncing forward on the wave face and jerking the boat down the front of the wave and then moving back to keep the nose out of the water. I say you can pump, which is frequent rapid trimming of the sail. This jerks the bow out of the water and initiates the plane. And I say you can rock, which achieves the same thing, breaking surface friction. Whether once on a plane you can continue in this pumping, ooching and rocking status is a real question.

I have never seen protests lodged against people who pump, ooch or rock while on a plane because the defense is pretty easy — they were just coming off the plane and had to go to these exertions on the new set of waves to get back planing again. Awfully hard to prove someone is wrong in this circumstance.

That's how you get on the plane. Make sure you keep your bow parallel to the water; that means going forward when you are headed down the face of the wave and back when you are headed up; don't sit so far back that your nose begins to come up. This creates much more drag because of the increased wetted surface at the stern. Sit in the middle, keep the boat level, and pump like hell.

But whatever you do, when you get that puff, give your sail a little pump, maybe even come up a little to get your speed up, and then bear off and run with the new breeze. Then come back up in the lulls, off in the puffs, etc. Nowhere is the Manfred Curry maxim of up in the lulls and off in the puffs more important than in reaching in oscillating winds. As long as you keep your air clear, follow this rule all the way down the reaching leg.

If you are in very light conditions there are other techniques to employ; these will be covered in the chapter on running.

There is the type of reach which is maddening to many sailors, known as the one leg beat. The object on a close reach is to be ahead and to leeward. Then, whichever way the wind switches you gain. If the wind stays steady then occasionally the boat out on your weather quarter may fetch whatever mark you are seeking and you will have to take a short hitch; but usually, be ahead and to leeward.

Now we are almost at the end of our reach. We have held low and we are closing with the rest of the group. Size up the rounding situation. Are you going to get the inside overlap? If so, hail the outside yachts that you are overlapped and that you will require room. If they are ahead but are approaching the mark at an angle which permits you the overlap, keep going.

If, however, you are ahead of them, slow down enough to maintain the overlap certainly, but the best tactical position you can have rounding the reaching mark and heading for the leeward mark is to be slightly ahead and to weather. This is even more true when rounding the leeward mark.

If you have not achieved the overlap, keep going. Don't give up. Sometimes boats ahead slow down when they get within 10 lengths or so and do a little housekeeping preparatory to the next leg; you can occasionally get the overlap at the last legal minute.

However, if you are not going to get the room, slow down, watch the situation. Regularly in large fleets money is made on the "slow down and win" principle. In a crowd, be the first or last at the reaching mark. As many boats get involved that turning circle gets wider and wider and sometimes a lively hole appears right at the mark for the crafty opportunist to drive into.

So far we have been talking about steady breezes and planing conditions. Shifty airs present a more challenging and interesting reaching condition. First and most important, look for puffs. The Long Island Sound premise of reach to the new breeze is paramount to fast off-wind sailing. Being to weather in a shifting wind is preferable to staying low. Sometimes the wind swings forward and you are blanketing the leeward boat. Also the boat to weather gets the new breeze first.

Remember, then:

Keep your air clear.
Plan the reach ahead of time.
Stay low.
Up in the lulls, off in the puffs.
Look for opportunities at marks.
Concentrate.
Pump, ooch and rock to get on that plane.
Sail the boat flat.

# RUNNING

The greatest downwind sailor in small boats today is Jeorg Bruder. Studying him in binoculars spectators say he moves about in the boat at least twice as much as most of the regular Sunfish sailors, squeezing every last inch out of the waves and puffs.

In contrast, I sail downwind in big seas and heavy winds with the basic intent of avoiding a capsize. This is not winning sailing. In a screamer, downwind work is frightening, but if you remember two principles things will become easier for you. If you sit to weather, as your normal tendency might be, you don't balance too well on this point of sail and sometimes begin the death roll. If you think you are going to capsize to weather, haul in the sheet; amazingly, you will come up level. I am convinced that the fastest course downwind in a breeze is just this — a succession of near windward capsizes. I don't have quite the courage to practice this regularly.

The other basic idea is to sail the boat level and frequently by the lee depending on the wave formation. The sail does develop a nicer shape when it is by the lee.

The slowest point of sail is dead downwind. Some sharp sailors have luck in jibing downwind. I have sailed at least 1,000 races in the last few years. I have almost never seen jibing downwind pay — mainly because Sunfish courses are so short.

Don't misunderstand, I have seen people hold low and be the last one to jibe over and ultimately gain ground, but jibing out of a fleet and jibing back? Rarely. Just stay in the parade — low if you can, playing the puffs as on a reach, watch your masthead fly, keep your air clear.

Wave riding off wind is important. Remember that wave crests are moving at as much as 20 knots, so get on the face of a wave and do everything you can to stay there. Your sail may luff but that isn't important. When the sail luffs keep playing it, this is certainly legal even though you are surfing, since you are adjusting for the natural action of the wind and waves.

Some of the best people are able to ooch the boat forward to take advantage of the last few yards of the wave face. As the boat begins to slow, through the wave running out from under you, throw yourself forward a couple of times and sometimes the stern picks up and you can get right back on the wave again and keep planing.

There are times when you go faster than the wave, usually because you are not going straight down it. If that is so, slow up by putting down the board or sitting aft a little so that you can stay on the wave. The key is to stay on the wave because if you move out ahead of it you go into a trough and it is hard to get back onto even the next wave.

Naturally, pumping, rocking and ooching are critical to promote surfing. Look behind you; when you see the wave approaching, move quickly forward, get the stern out of the water and when the wave catches you, sit as far forward as you can and not broach.

The trouble with the Sunfish downwind is that the rudder is not deep enough and the boat becomes extremely hard to

steer dead before the wind. I try to sail across the wind as much as possible, still following the puffs down.

The Sunfish has broaching troubles. The way to eliminate them is to balance the boat so that you are precariously close to nose diving, but can shift your weight aft, even jump on the stern to keep the bow out. Sail a little by the lee too.

If you start broaching, bounce on the stern, steer up and when the bow comes out of the water like a whale, bear sharply off, otherwise you will keep coming up and substantially lose your course, and maybe capsize.

In light air it is a different game — one of patience and cunning. Really, you want to keep your sails full and driving. Remember the drawing on page 61. It shows the halyard being tied to the tack. Pulling on the halyard while sitting to windward keeps the sails cocked up, full, while still reducing wetted surface. Keep the board up as much as you can and still be able to steer. Do not pull the board out of the trunk; you are asking for increased drag due to water entering the trunk.

You might consider pulling up the rudder and trailing it at the ready but not in the water. This is particularly true and valuable when there are weedy conditions. Experiment with the tension on the rudder. You should be able to pop it free of the latch plate simply by banging the tiller down on the deck.

Make sure you are alert to conditions of tide, and current. Needless to say downwind sailing which is slow to begin with is even more deadly when you are in an adverse current. If you can, stay to the side of the course and reach over to the mark at the last minute.

Just remember that everyone is going relatively slowly downwind, and if you can take advantage of angles and sail a scalloped, reaching course, your chances of gaining distance are good.

# TEAM RACING

Team racing is the most rewarding of all sailboat racing efforts. It brings out the character and quality in all of us. It requires an intimate knowledge of the rules and the most encompassing application of tactics in yacht racing. It is a sport in which old slow grey heads can excel against the young bucks with boat speed.

Basically, team racing is a contest between two groups of equal numbers of boats, usually four or five. The object is simply to place your boats across the finish line in a sequence which will give you fewer aggregate points than the other team. Twenty seven is the maximum low point total required in a five boat team race; 18 in a four boat race. On the water it is easier to add low points than to remember the combinations. We won't delve into mathematical computations here, but needless to say placing 1,2 does not insure a win in five boat racing. Team balance such as in a 3,4,5,7,8 is more important. You might tape the list of winning combinations to your boat.

It is rare that anyone agrees on starting techniques let alone regularly executes them. However, we have had astonishing success by assigning positions along the line — one man as the hatchet at the starboard end cutting off bargers and the rest spread out. If each man knows his place and sticks to it during a series, a pattern begins to form and teamwork is maximized.

Freelancing is frequently used. This theory usually implies that you are a team with superior speed. After the start you should be ahead and each man then sits on an opponent. This method is similar to man-for-man coverage in basketball as opposed to zone defense.

If the line favors the port end, one of the favorite tactics of Chuck and Teddy Moore is to luff the opponent nearest the pin to the point where Teddy can get a port tack start. In team racing a quarter point bonus is paid for a first place and it is even more important than to try to spring a fast sailor clear.

Another favorite trick against a team with two or three very strong sailors is for your slowest men to tail the hot shots of the other team away from the line or to luff them over the line prematurely.

Once out on the course the object is to stay in contact with the opponents. It is all well and good to sail fast but the wind does funny things. Leads of 100 yards evaporate quickly in a 45 degree wind shift. Generally speaking you should cover both sides of the course. Man-to-man coverage is important, but not to the point of inflexibility.

Passing an opponent from one teammate to another makes sense. As an example, teammate A is on starboard, crossing teammate B sailing on port. B is covering opponent C, also on port. C tacks to break the cover and B lets him go as A is already on the same tack.

Communication is extremely important on the water. You must talk to each other; and if you think the Venezuelans don't have an advantage when they scheme in Spanish you have one more think coming.

Upwind the most effective tactic is to blanket an opponent. The rules now permit sailing down on an enemy as long as you don't touch him. Another effective maneuver is to sail a dangerous man past the lay line. In team racing there is no proper course requirement on an upwind leg. There is therefore no requirement that a boat on another's weather quarter tack for the mark until both have overstood and it is safe to go for it. Remember, however, when you are jockeying against a boat on another leg of the course, you must sail a course considered proper for your own leg.

The weather mark presents good opportunities to help break some teammates through. As mentioned you can stay on a yacht's weather quarter until your teammates have rounded. If you are inside boat and have luffing rights, you may sail on past the required side of the mark without ever laying off for the next mark. And naturally if you are outside boat with luffing rights and hail outside two boat lengths, you can take an overlapping boat on the wrong side of the mark. This is very effective due to its surprise element. While this stipulation is a part of the regular rules of racing it is very seldom used because you usually are more concerned with the fleet rather than a single man.

Reaching and running afford many opportunities to hold opponents off to the betterment of teammates. The same mark rounding rules apply as on weather legs. Luffing head to wind is a tactic frequently used. Remember the creed, however: yacht racing is a sport of gentlemen. The object is not, and never should be, to touch another yacht out of the race. There is no fun in sailing against undermanned teams. It requires more skill to interfere legally with another yacht than it does to foul out someone.

Both upwind and downwind finishes are exciting in team racing. Always assess the point score before crossing. It is a relatively easy trick on an upwind finish to wait for an opponent and blanket him in hopes of slipping a teammate through. It is somewhat more difficult and therefore more challenging to help out on a downwind finish.

If you foul out, withdraw promptly. I have known only one sailor who felt he stayed in a race and made money even with his four point penalty. It is almost an impossibility.

Most team races which end in ties are resolved in scoring by beaten teams (if both of us lost one race but I beat you and lost to some other team which lost more than once, then I win). But sometimes they are settled by total points in the series. It is all the more important to be unselfish and sacrifice one's own position if it is to the ultimate advantage of the team.

At Darien we run off more than 75 team races a weekend during the Nationals. Identification of the boats is achieved either through colored shirts for the competitors, pennants on the leeches of the sails or decals on the Sunfish on the sail. Naturally, courses tend to get cluttered with that many boats. It is unlikely that other classes will face the complex problem, but if they do, they might consider the uniquely modified Gold Cup course which got groups off to the side for their second beat and downwind finish.

Team racing truly adds a new dimension to sailing. Lots of team races on short courses really sharpen up your techniques and tactical senses. We believe that in a few years team racing will be a part of many major singlehand regattas.

# FROSTBITING

Most of my business friends are now thoroughly convinced that I am absolutely out of my mind. To give up the comforts of Sunday afternoon in front of the TV set? To miss the delights of the neighborhood saloon? Or how can your wife let you go on winter Sundays when she knows full well no work will get done around the house come spring? And then for what? To sit for two or three hours with your tail dragging in freezing water, slush forming in the cockpit and spray turning your cheeks to icicles? Oh what fun.

And I nod contentedly to myself. I have something to achieve each Sunday afternoon. I can race my boat. The pleasures of winter sailing far exceed the discomforts, and unless you capsize, the discomforts are really minimal.

Traditionally frostbite sailing is done in Interclubs, Penguins or Dyers. Only in recent years has the Sunfish gained in popularity as a frostbite boat. The objection to the boat used to be that you were so close to the water when you sat on the deck. The idea was that for a winter boat you needed a high freeboard. Now people have come to recognize that it is exactly because of the high sides that the traditional dinghies are not proper frostbite boats. How many times have you seen a capsized Dyer get up and sail the same day? Usually they are towed home half submerged, incurring some breakage along the way. Conversely the Sunfish pops right up, permitting its skipper to sail again immediately — if he hasn't congealed.

Further, the normal dinghy just doesn't sail in 20 knot breezes. I know there are some exceptions, but generally speaking the dinghies cannot go in much over 20. On the protected waters where most frostbite races are sailed, it takes 30 knots to blow out a Sunfish race. Indeed, Sunfish are even raced in conditions of 35-50 when waters are warmer. The Sunfish is a far more stable boat and has much more speed than the traditional boat. It has even made inroads as the frostbite boat used in Narragansett Bay, which is very much dinghy country.

Riverside Yacht Club in Connecticut is one of the more formal yacht clubs in the East. It was with some trepidation that the club management permitted the Sunfish to be raced with the Dyers. In deference to the seniority of the Dyer they still start the slower boat first.

Commodore Emeritus Clifton Hipkins has said repeatedly that the Sunfish has emerged as the best frostbite boat on the Sound. The numbers of dinghy sailors switching to the Sunfish are increasing each year.

Now that you are sailing the right boat you had better dress properly. If I know we are going to get a sea, I wear a one piece foul weather suit, but with sweat pants and shirt over it so that I do not slide unnecessarily. The best garment would be a wet suit. Usually, however, I wear my long underwear, pants, shirts and sweaters so that I have mobility.

I think the best gloves are rubber coated work gloves. Most people find that in the excitement of racing they don't wear gloves and just put them on in the interval between races.

Bob Bowles came up with a good idea for keeping the feet warm. He uses a thin pair of socks over which he slips a plastic sandwich bag. Another pair of socks and Topsider boots complete the outfit. I find boots cumbersome and just use a pair of Topsider moccasins.

A Navy watch cap is good headgear and a turtle neck sweater is in order when there is a good breeze.

With this gear I stay warm and find that I never have any problems with the weather.

Most well organized clubs will not go without two crash boats, which is quite important. Frequently two boats will go over under a particularly vicious puff and you need two rescue vessels. The best rule has it that should a boat capsize, the race is immediately called off and everyone goes to the scene of the accident. There is some debate about this. I have never seen a sailor who is behind in the race deliberately capsize so that his series standing won't be impaired but I really wouldn't put it past some of us.

Usually frostbite races operate under two minute starts. This works so well I wonder why we don't go this route for racing other times of the year. Frostbite courses are usually quite short and that's fun. Long races in a Sunfish test other skills but lots of short races are really more rewarding because of the greater intellectual challenge. You get much more expert in application of rules and tactics when you have so many more opportunities to practice.

People wondered at the great improvement in the American group in 1970. One of the reasons I am sure is because we race so many short courses that our starting techniques have sharpened up; we are learning to get away in clear air.

We store our boats in the open at Riverside on lovely cradles right on the dock. It is a first class situation. You should put on a boat cover. Don't leave sails, boards, rudders on the boat during the week for obvious reasons. If you do not have a cover, put a tennis ball in the mast well. Chopping out a solid tube of ice from the trunk when your competitors are milling about on the starting line is not one of the things I like about frostbiting. A cover prevents ice from forming in the cockpit. If it does, however, you can easily get it out if you are neat and a little patient. Pour some hot water around the edges and then chip with a hammer and screwdriver in a straight line away from an edge. The whole block will usually fall apart in two pieces. Make sure you drain your boat after every day. Don't let ice form inside during the week. Take the extra trouble to fresh water rinse after each sail.

Winter sailing really is glorious. You are outside in fresh air, competing fairly with decent people. You are active, stimulated by the excitement of the challenge. And after the boats are put away, you can still get a little bit of that neighborhood saloon bit in too. I think it's a lot more fun than watching Namath and his cast walking up and down the sidelines. And now there is Monday night football anyway.

# MAINTENANCE

The joy of having the boat surge underneath you, literally bouncing over the waves, is something else again. And it is in recollection of the buoyancy that the knowledge that you are being both outpointed and outfooted becomes such a sickening feeling. Many times the trouble does not lie with the skipper but with the boat itself — you may be leaking. It is amazing to me that Alcort is able to mass produce so many boats and have so few that leak. But ultimately after long use, these constructions will leak.

Naturally you should regularly check for water. If any develops here is what to do.

Mix a solution of one part water to one part detergent — really sudsy. Get a couple of pieces of scotch tape. Use one to tape over the air vent in the front wall of the cockpit. Open the drain plug and blow in hard several times. When you think you have built up good pressure, tape over the drain plug.

Now slowly draw a paint brush loaded with soap suds over the danger parts of the boat:

All along the aluminum edging

The mast trunk

The daggerboard trunk

The rudder assembly

If you have a leak, the suds will bubble up. Still no bubbles? Keep going.

Inside the cockpit where the deck joins the tub

All the screw holes

Under the rudder latch

At the bow

You should have found any leak by now. But if you haven't inspect the actual bottom of the boat, sometimes hairline fractures develop which go unnoticed on a cursory inspection.

Once you have located the troubles, repairs are pretty easy, thanks to the miracles of epoxy resins. Chuck is the expert in this field. After teaching ninety kids each summer at Wequaquet Lake Yacht Club, where the main sport for the young is to sink the other kids, he learned to repair boats or he would not have had any classes the next day.

He advises the following:

Before you repair any part, make sure it is clean.

If the leak is in the mast trunk at the lip, rout around the lip and fill in with epoxy. Actually he uses Marine Tex which applies beautifully and sands better, but is expensive. Any epoxy will do.

If your problem is at the bottom of the trunk, pour a liquid epoxy, such as offered by Sears in its marine department, into the bottom of the well. Make sure the boat is level and the resin will settle evenly.

The daggerboard trunk should be treated in the same fashion, routing out the damaged area and filling with Marine Tex. A little wet sanding and you are in business.

Marine Tex the area around the trim if a leak has developed there.

The time will come when some intrepid port tacker will try

to take out his frustrations on you and stick his bow through your side. If you can make it ashore you will be all right and back sailing the next day.

First, sand around the hole and remove all loose pieces of gelcoat. Make the hole large enough to work with.

Then cut out a piece of cardboard an inch larger than the hole in the boat. Also cut a matching piece of fiberglass cloth.

Put a piece of string a foot long through a hole in the center of the cardboard and fiberglass cloth. Tie a knot at the end of the line opposite the cloth.

Mix epoxy resin and paint the cloth, bonding it to the cardboard. Put the cloth and cardboard inside the hole, drawing this patch to the hull with the other end of the string. Fit the patch to the hull. Tie the string to any heavy object by the side of the boat in order to maintain pressure while the resin hardens. Once the epoxy solidifies, cut the string, and fill the depression with a filler such as Marine Tex. Paste or tape a piece of clear polyethylene tape over the entire patch and smooth it with a putty knife, wiping off the squeezings which seep under the tape. The result will be a nice smooth patch almost not requiring sanding, and one which can easily be painted over.

As mentioned, the rivets occasionally pop loose and they are easily fixed by drilling a new hole and using the pop rivet gun to insert new rivets.

Those of you who trail the boats regularly will ultimately have the problem of the cockpit lip beginning to give, showing some tell tale cracks. This can be reinforced by use of a piece of 1½ inch cardboard tube cut in half in 24 inch strips. Bond pieces of fiberglass cloth to the tube with epoxy. These pieces should be six inches wide. The boat should be placed upside down and level. Place the tube with the cloth to the underside of the lip, with the semicircle of the tube facing the lip. Let this cure and the reinforcement will work.

Just keep checking regularly for water. It must appear at some time and when it does you can rest in confidence that you can repair the leaks.

## DO'S AND DON'TS

Sunfish sailors are usually relatively new to the sport. Yachting is one of the most exacting of all athletic endeavors in regard to ethics and character. Over the years we have embarrassed ourselves with foolish, ungentlemanly actions and seen other people make similar errors of judgment.

We are going to attempt in a few words to describe the type of person whom we would like to sail with, and who will be invited by all clubs to join in their activities.

Do enjoy yourself; don't make the sport so competitive that you lose sight of the fact that it is a game.

Do sail by the rules; don't violate the rules to the extent that you could not tell your son what you did on the race course.

Do protest when you have been fouled by someone trying to take deliberate advantage of the situation; don't be protest-happy and protest any and all comers regardless of the nature of the foul or the outcome of the series.

Do drop out when you have fouled; don't wait hoping that good hearted or soft hearted Joe won't protest you or that the race committee will miraculously throw out all protests.

Speak kindly to your competitors on the water; don't scream at a beginner to get out of your way and maybe lose a potential competitor forever.

DO SAIL IT FLAT.

# REGATTA CHECKLIST

## You must have:

| | | | |
|---|---|---|---|
| Sail | Boat | Rudder | Board |
| Sheet | Mast | Spars | Halyard |
| Life jacket | Rudder pin | Bailing plug, marble gasket | |

## You really should not be without:

| | | | |
|---|---|---|---|
| Tell tales | Bailer | Sponge | Boots |
| Sweat shirts | Gloves | Topsiders | Hat |
| Sweat pants | Detergent | Rule book | Appeals |
| Foul weather gear | | | |

## And in your tool box:

| | | | |
|---|---|---|---|
| Pop rivet gun | Marine Tex | Extra yard | Cap nuts |
| S Hook | Rubber bands | Hammer | No. 10 wire |
| Screw driver | Tape | Pliers | Knife |
| Hand drill | Bits | Screws and bolts | |
| Wet sand paper | Silicone seal | Extra outhaul line | |
| Tape measure | Extra sail sets | Telephone, toll money | |

# GLOSSARY

Not too many years ago I used sailing books as a bromide; I would read a chapter and by the end I would be asleep. I simply didn't understand all of the complicated terminology. If you have trouble with this book, I understand. Sleep well. This glossary attempts to make just as clear as possible all of the terms that a relative newcomer might have some trouble with. My son, a fairly new sailor, has read the book. When he comes to something he doesn't grasp, we note and include it in this glossary. If a term does not appear here, a quick reference to the definitions in the NAYRU Racing Rules would get you the answer.

**Blanket**
Interfere with the air of another yacht from a windward position.

**Bob Bowles**
Garden City, N.Y. Past Commodore, D.S.Y.R.A. Runner-up 1971 World's Championship.

**Broach**
When the boat submerges its bow and rounds up to weather, losing way and often capsizing.

**Broad Reach**
A faster point of sail than with the wind dead aft. The wind is not blowing perpendicular to the fore and aft line of the boat, as this is defined as a "beam reach." Nor is the wind blowing forward of the perpendicular line, which is described as a "close reach."

**Doug Brown**
Miami, Fla. 1968 Midwinter Champion.

**Bob Bushnell**
Darien, Conn. My teacher, both of technique and tactics, and, more importantly, of sailing ethics. Won everything in sight when competing regularly in class. Now winning everything on Wall Street.

**Clew**
That part of the sail on the foot which is tied to the outer end of the boom.

**Bruce Connolly**
V.P. and General Manager AMF-Alcort. Built the company.

**Skip Cook**
Mint Hill Station, N.C. Founder of D.S.Y.R.A. One of the most imaginative and inventive of all Sunfish sailors.

**Manfred Curry**
The father of modern sailing theory. Wrote "The Aerodynamics of Sails."

**Draft**
The deep curvature of the sail, or camber.

**Jack Evans**
Smoke Rise, N.J. U.S. Sailfish Champion three years in succession.

**Flat**
The name of the game. When the boat is upright and level to the water, rather than heeled over.

**Jon Freeman**
Cos Cob, Conn. One of the best of the Long Island Sound "pros."

**Gooseneck**
The ring on the boom through which the mast fits.

**Dick Griffin**
St. Thomas, U.S. Virgin Islands. N.A. Champion 1970. Keen student of the game and lovable personality.

**Headed**
When the wind shifts forward of you rather than to the side or back as in a "lift."

**Hike**
That condition of physical involvement which finds the skipper and/or crew with the majority of his weight held outside the boat on the windward side in an effort to balance and hold the boat level. Usually one is suspended by his toes under the far side of the cockpit although shorter people have to tuck their feet under the fore and aft sections of the cockpit. An exhausting yet satisfying physical exertion.

**Bob Holzman**
Morrisville, Pa. Founder D.S.Y.R.A. Heavy weather ace.

**Harvey Howell**
San Juan, Puerto Rico, 1971 Caribbean Midwinter Champion and ace guy.

**Garry Hoyt**
1970 Sunfish World Champion, of San Juan, Puerto Rico. Manager of Domestic Operations, Young & Rubicam, Inc.

**IYRU**
The International Yacht Racing Union.

### Bob Johnstone
Wilmette, Ill. N.A. Penguin Champion 1969. Introduced the class to many of the tuning techniques considered standard today.

### Ken Klein
St. Thomas, U.S. Virgin Islands, fourth at 1970 World's Championships.

### Carl Knight
Mamaroneck, New York. 1969 N. A. Champion. Commodore D.S.Y.R.A.

### Jack Knights
London, England. One-Design & Offshore Yachtsman Magazine's European correspondent. Multi-class competitor.

### Lateen Rig
That's what the Sunfish rig is, a sail bounded by two spars raised on an unstayed mast.

### Layline
If you steer along this line close hauled you can just fetch, or clear, the windward mark.

### Leech
The hypotenuse of the triangle of the sail shape. The line between the top of the sail and the outer boom end.

### Lift
When the wind comes from behind you. Or, when you are sailing upwind on starboard tack and the wind shifts even further to the right (sailing upwind on port tack and the wind shifts even further to the left).

### Luff
The forward edge of the sail, from top to bottom. As a verb, "to luff" means to alter one's course to windward to a point where the sail begins to shake or flap.

### Luffing Rights
The low (leeward) boat can force the high (windward) boat up into the wind as far as he pleases on the same tack until the helmsman of the upwind boat is forward of the mast of the luffing boat. See Yacht Racing Rules of the North American Yacht Racing Union.

**John Magenheimer**
1966 Sailfish Champion.

**Mainsheet Block**
The lead through which the mainsheet winds. The pulley on this device gives a mechanical advantage.

**Marginal Planing**
When the lightweight kids can scoot along on the waves and most of us wallow in the troughs, never getting enough of the boat out of the water to take advantage of the surfing action of the waves.

**Teddy Moore**
Cornell University Senior, member Cape Cod Plus YRA and, most importantly, 1971 World Sunfish Champion.

**NAYRU**
The North American Yacht Racing Union.

**Overlap**
When your bow is ahead of a perpendicular line drawn through the end of the rudder (not the end of the transom).

**Pinching**
That which we all should not do: sailing the boat on too high an angle to the wind. Difficult to detect when you are doing it. Boat slows down even though sails are still filled.

**Mike Shaw**
Tortola, British Virgin Islands. Sailed England to St. Thomas in home-constructed boat. 1970 World's Runner-up. Alpine climber.

**Sheet**
The rope or line with which you trim the sails.

**Palmer Sparkman**
Riverside, Conn. 1970 L.I.S. Soling Champion.

**Tack**
Changing course upwind (bringing bow across wind so that sail fills on other side). Is also variously defined as the course you are on. (Starboard tack means that the wind is blowing from the starboard side of the boat. One is able to tack downwind, but the usual expression is to jibe downwind.) "Tack" also means that corner of the sail which is affixed to the juncture of the spars.

**Rudy Thompson**
St. Thomas, U.S. Virgin Islands. Founder of World Class competition.

**Sandy Traub**
Millville, N.J. Regular New Jersey hot shot.

**Vang**
A device used to hold the boom down to flatten the sail. Also keeps the boom from riding up in a chop to maintain an even airflow off the sail.

**Wetted Surface**
That portion of the hull which comes in contact with the water. The heavier the skipper, the greater the wetted surface.

**Will White**
Hartford, Conn. N.A. Champion 1968 and 1966.

**Ward Young**
Hamilton, Bermuda. Inventor of "Sail It Flat." One of the original Sunfish devotees.